SPIRITUAL THOUGHTS

by
Robert Brant

CON-PSY PUBLICATIONS MIDDLESEX

First Edition

© Robert Brant
1998

Published by

CON-PSY PUBLICATIONS

P.O. BOX 14,
GREENFORD,
MIDDLESEX, UB6 0UF.

ISBN 1 898680 14 0

INDEX

My Dedication.

Many years ago, before the war, a mother gave birth to a very special baby, this baby grew up and became my wife, Her mother, a very dear lady, whom I admired very much, was also very special. She not only had the gift of insight and foresight, but possessed the very essence of spirituality, although she would not have seen it that way. The essence is explained this way. All through her life, not taking into account the ups and downs, which are part and parcel of our physical lives, she was a giver and never a taker. This fine spiritual attribute, made her stand out amongst others. It's very hard giving, all of the time,especially when extremely poor. It was not money that was the key factor in her life, although she would give that too, it was the ability of giving of herself. This was her self worth, this spiritual force was with her throughout her entire life, God bless her, and I was privileged to have known her for a few years. She always treated me as one of her own, and never as an outsider. She was very happy that I had met her daughter, her only child and that her daughter and I were very happy together. I instantly felt a part of their family, and that's the way it stayed.

My wife and I moved to Bletchley, Bucks, and Bletchley was soon to become a part of the now Milton Keynes. All the way through our married life, my wife who inherited this special gift from her mother, really began to shine. Our son Donald also possesses this gift, of giving, but at this time no insight. When we moved to Bletchley, we had come from London, and Bletchley was an over-spill town. We lived quite happily for several years in our council house. This remarkable gift that my wife Betty possessed, soon started to rub off onto our local neighbours. There was always laughter in our house and a feeling of goodwill to who ever called. You could not help in liking this bubbly blond, who with me got involved in local committees, and Betty the estate paper. We eventually moved to another house in Bletchley and this was our first own house. Betty had been working for a big named bank, and had enjoyed her work, and all the fun that went with it. She met and became friends with many of them, until this day. After her work had finished,she became a full time housewife and mother.

She also helped me, when in the early eighties I started our business. She was an asset, because she possessed that instant appeal, when talking on the telephone to our customers and suppliers, it helped me in establishing a business that lasted several years. Now that we were on a higher income,we moved yet again, this time to a larger house, but it was the house setting that impressed Betty, and it overcome her fear that we had stepped up, too high, too quick, the year was 1984. In 1981, Betty was admitted to hospital, for a planned operation to remove her spleen. If we had only known then what future outcomes would be, as a direct result of that operation. Although she had been in and out of hospital, she still kept smiling, even though in pain. In 1986, Betty after suffering from very bad headaches for a number of years, suffered an Aneurysm, which is a burst blood vessel in the brain, and this was to become years of increasing suffering for her. The point of me telling you about my wives suffering, is this, that in all that time she did not once weaken her resolve in helping others, in laughter, or as a hospital volunteer, with the same result. It took her two years, to make a full recovery from this. At the end of her recovery, she developed shingles, with all the pain and stress that go's with that, and still smiled and joked. While suffering from shingles, she developed acute Glaucoma and was rushed once again to hospital, after an operation to save her sight, in one eye, she was still smiling through the pain. It always lifted my heart when visiting her in hospital. She came home again and all was well for a while. In 1991 she fell over the dogs beany bag, which was on the floor in the hall, she had got up herself, before I reached her, and with my help, limped into the lounge. After seating her in the armchair, I called the Doctor on call out, and it happened to be my friend. He came in and looked at Betty sitting in the chair and asked her to stand, and as she could, he felt it was just internal bruising, how wrong he was. She dragged herself about for almost a week, and kept saying to me that she was all right. In the end I could not stand it any longer and called an ambulance. When the paramedic entered the room, he took one look and said that her hip was fractured. At this time I had just started my training as a spiritual healer. She spent the next two weeks in hospital, and was bolted back together again. While there she astounded some of the medical staff, with her mediumship, often having a queue of nurses and doctors, waiting for a reading.

She was then exhausted by she time I got there for my visit. My friend meanwhile was quite upset about the wrong diagnosis, that he made, but we forgave him. Apart from the pain my wife suffered in her leg after the fracture, we had a relatively quiet two years. From 1993 she suffered from many problems, starting with Septicemia, another two weeks in hospital. From all the illness that she suffered from at this time, spiritual healing was given each time, and she always sprang back from it. The smiling and general happiness continued, for all that were around her. She had her own kind of wit, that always brought a smile to the glumness face. She was to visit hospital a few more times yet. With a couple of bouts of pneumonia, all due to her inability, to fight off germs etc. Which is a direct result in having the spleen removed, lessening the amount of immunity your body can fight with. On one of her visits, she was asked, when did you develop

Angina, her answer to this was, I've never had Angina. No more was said to her, until the next visit, when she was admitted after collapsing with a heart problem, this time it was Fibrillation. The heart beating at a fast rate of knots. This was now towards the end of 1995, her average heart beat was 110 to the minute, this condition was to remain with her. Betty was given various drugs to try and steady the heart, to aid it, through her life. With this she started to develop Emphysema, and after a heart scan, she was found to have heart disease of both valves. This condition is normally operable, but in her case, not so. We have to return back to the spleen once more. The spleen was removed because of a platelet shortage in her blood, and although it helped her condition at that time, it prevented her from having heart surgery, Most of the tests were carried out in 1996. In the beginning of 1997, new years day in fact, she had to return to hospital again, with heart problems and two weeks stay, Betty still remained cheerful through out this ordeal, with spiritual and medical healing she came home till June.

In between those months, she was quite well. In June she went in again, heart related for nine days. While she was in there, she made friends with two of the other patients. After they had all been at home for a while, they kept in regular contact with each other, often having a laugh on the telephone. It was soon after this time that my wife and I were talking one evening, an she said something that alarmed me, and didn't really want to hear. This is what she said, I need to tell you something Bob, I will not be here Christmas, with hearing that and at the same time knowing that when she forecasted anything it was always right, I said to her oh don't be silly, I'll probably go long before you. She said know more to me about it and it left me frightened. We did, as we normally do, our Christmas shopping at the beginning of November, she enjoyed being pushed about in her wheel chair, and we went to the city centre and bought some presents for our son. We had a very enjoyable day and then returned home. Everything seemed fine and normal again. life continued as much as did before, but this all changed on November 19th, at five twenty in the morning Betty called out to me Bob I've fallen. She had gone to the toilet and as she went to walk away, she had a sudden stroke. Once again back to the hospital, she had paralysis down the left side, she could speak, but with a slur. She was admitted, but because of a shortage of beds, was placed in a surgical ward.

The staff on this ward were wonderful and every few minutes were coming round to see if Betty was all right. She stayed on this ward for two weeks, an while on this ward, had the staff and patients in fits of laughter. On one occasion that I visited her, she said to me, that Lisa our daughter-in-law had bought her a pair of bed socks, at this time because of bad circulation, several parts of her body were cold, anyway apparently she had played the same Joke on each sister of each shift. So she said that's the sister over there, I'll call her over, she said sister, sister come quickly, my feet have gone blue and knobbly, she came rushing over, pulled back the bedclothes, and saw light blue bed socks with knobbly bits on. Everyone laughed, it was a very magical moment. When Betty fell with the stroke she injured her left thumb, and a part of her wrist, there was a huge swelling there, so while she was dozing, I gave her healing, the very next day the swelling had gone and the pain with it. On the first night that she was in there, I asked a couple of friends who were themselves healers, to do a joint absent healing at nine o'clock that evening, we did, the next day Betty was able to fully bend her left leg and move her toes, also her little finger. I was very pleased for her. She looked very happy and bright, on the twelfth day, the sister on the ward phoned me and asked if I could bring the dogs over for Betty to see. We have two cocker spaniel's, o.a.ps now, They allowed me to take them into the ward and onto her bed, mud and kisses everywhere, it made her day an mine. On the fourteenth day she was transferred to a stroke re-hab ward, where she met a couple of nurses who had worked with Betty when she was an active volunteer. This cheered her up knowing that there was someone there she new. On the sixteenth day, a dear friend who is in charge of the hospital volunteers, our Rosie came and visited Betty, They had quite a chin-wag,and what she had said to Rosie, I was to learn about less than a week later.

I arrived, as Rosie was leaving. Betty now looked very unwell,she had caught a bladder infection and was being treated for it. Since being in hospital, she had not eaten any solids, because mainly she did feel sick in the stomach, and half of her mouth was not working properly. When she did take even drinks, it was 50/50 whether or not it would reach her stomach, because some of it went down into her lungs, This caused her severe wind problems with the feeling of indigestion, on every visit she would sit forward and have her back rubbed and with luck release some of it. I was encouraged by the staff, in trying to feed her, normally milk or orange juice, I had to chart it each day to show how much she had had. On the seventeenth, eighteenth and nineteenth day she was very ill, she had a drip feeding into her arm, her breathing had become erratic. I was now more than at any other time very worried, I stayed late with her each evening, giving healing there and absent when I would eventually get home. On the twentyth day she seemed slightly better, after trying to feed her, I read a part of a book to her, we spent the rest of the time cuddling and holding hands. Because my Betty had problems swallowing, her mouth would normally be bunged up, and each evening I would help her to clear it. Well on this night her mouth was completely clear, so instead of kissing her goodbye on the forehead, we kissed each other on the lips, I waved as I was leaving her sight,she waved back and said thanks for coming, I said see you tomorrow. The next day my lovely Betty passed over, after suffering a massive heart attack, they tried in vain to bring her back. This was her prophecy, her destiny. My life was left with a gaping hole in it, her funeral, was one week exactly before Christmas day 1997.

Although I possess spiritual knowledge of the higher levels, and I thought that I would handle this situation differently, I could not, this I admit to you all. Rosie came round to see me, she offered me her dedication of Betty to me, and asked if I would use some of it in the talk that I gave at the funeral, I used all of it. Betty in all of her life that she spent with me, was dedicated in bringing as much joy as possible to other people, when she was unable to walk anymore, she would sit for hours knitting dolls, of all shapes and sizes. Little character people type dolls, which were enjoyable to look at, these in turn were used as raffle prizes, to raise money to buy the training, of guide dogs to the blind. Some were given to sick children and the Fraser day hospital near where we live. It was not only dolls, it was sometimes money, but most of all it was her time and limited energies, that was focused on other people. Betty is a truly gifted spiritual person, her whole life spent in the service of others, and I was privileged to be her husband. We have talked many times since her passing, she has helped me enormously with my feelings of loss. In spirit now she is free of all pain, with her lovely mother, father, our old dog Petra and cat Sam. I'm left now to care for our dogs Rolo who is nearly fourteen and Amy who is eleven, I love them both very much, as I have always loved my Betty with that very deep spiritual love.

Rosie told me, that on that day in hospital, Betty had told her, that her life was now over.

My Betty, among other things was a brilliant poet, and below is a poem that I found, but am not sure whether she wrote it.

The Sad years of Compassion.

What do you see? you ask, What do we see? What are we thinking, when looking at thee.

We may seem hard when we hurry or fuss but there are so many of you, so few of us.

We would like more time to sit near you and talk, to bath you, to feed you, to help you to walk.

To hear of your lives and the things you have done. Your childhood, your husband, your daughter, your son.

But time is against us, there's so much to do, patients so many, nurses so few.

8

We grieve when we see you, so sad and alone, nobody near you, no friends of your own.

We feel all your pain, and know of your fear, that nobody cares now your time is near.

But nurses are people with feelings as well and when we are together you'll often hear tell, of the dearest old gran in the very end bed, of a dear old dad and the things that he said.

We speak with compassion and love and feel sad, when we think of your life and the Joys you've had, when the time has arrived for you to depart, you leave us behind with an ache in our heart.

When you sleep the long sleep no more worry or care.

But there are other old people and we must be there, so please understand if we worry or fuss, but there are so many of you, so few of us.

In memory of Betty Frances Brant.

This is my dedication to my wife and mother Betty, until we meet again, at home in spirit.

Words should not matter for you or I, for we both have the secret of eternal joy, we will be together, for the rest of my life, until its my turn to return home, and into the arms of you my wife.

I would also like to dedicate this book to guides and teachers; Little Bear, Silver Fox, Tei Lei, Tejget, Joseph and Elijah.

Preface

Spiritual Thought, Robert Brant's First offering to the world of Spiritualist Literature, was written in the limited time he could snatch between running a small business, and being an active healer in the new City of Milton Keynes.

The manuscript you are about to read is a complete, untouched record of Spiritually inspired messages, as received by the author. After many weeks editing the original script, I was informed by Robert that I was changing 'the character of the script, and personality of the communicators, therefore the true messages received were not getting across.As it was his pen, along with his guides words which brought this paper to life, I have since returned the script- to its original form. Hence this read does not, comply with what most would term as pure English grammar. This does not, however, detract from the strong opinions, beliefs, thoughts and philosophy of the author and his spiritual advisors. Some of which differ to ours, but nevertheless, make for a very interesting read.

Matthew P Hutton
Reviews & Research
Psychic World.

Introduction

My name is Robert Brant, I live in the new city of Milton Keynes. I have never had until recently any inclination of writing a book. So with the help of spirit, this is my first attempt. I'm writing this book in my limited spare time, as I have a small business. This book has been written to the benefit of the reader, hopefully answering some of your questions, and knowing some of you will of had similar feelings to myself. I feel that there is great need for people's questions to be answered, I would like to see more Spiritualists hiring halls for this purpose. I hope in the future to be doing just that.

Each of you are already on your spiritual pathway, it started as soon as you were conceived, and will continue all your life. Some of you will achieve many things some will achieve nothing. It depends on what you're learning in this life. If you have gained a similar status as myself in this life, then perhaps like myself this is your last earthly life and are meant for a higher spiritual life, perhaps as a guide or a philosopher. My philosophy is to help all people or animals in either thought or deed all your life. Being a spiritual healer is to heal people who might dislike you, not everybody can do this, it takes a special person or in another way someone who is on a higher spiritual level. Who can rise above the everyday problems and keep your mind pure.

The words written in this book, have been given to me by my spirit guides to my own educational level. Spirit can and do communicate in all languages, they are there to help you with all your spiritual needs. They give you ideas for you to develop into something useful. Your mind is your spirit or soul if you prefer, the mind is not in the brain, your spirit is what makes you, your personality and character good or bad. Fortunately believe it or not, most people in this world are good all their lives and the spiritual help you can get is always on the love line. The bad will only be helped if they are going to change their ways. When the bad return to spirit they have to learn all the basics again, and are quickly returned to the earth plane, for a new life which may not be anywhere as good as the last one. But nevertheless they will learn and perhaps improve. it would be true to say that some of what's written here, I have yet to attain, we are all human and make mistakes. I sometimes swear like a trooper and can be argumentative, they are some of my bad points, some of the good are, a kind heart, not greedy or materialistic. Helping others in deed when I can, in thought every day. So there is hope for us all.

Chapter One : In The Beginning

In the beginning there was light, the light being a spiritual presence in my bedroom. I was awakened by a burning sensation on the back of my neck. As I gradually awoke, my first feeling was that the house was on fire. There was an orange glow on the wall that I was facing. I started to sniff the air for smoke but there was none. I turned over onto my back, still unsure what was happening. I turned my head slightly to the left and there in between the pillows was an orange ball of light. My wife slept soundly unaware of what was happening. The hairs on the back of my neck stood to attention, I was in absolute fear. The light remained for about five minutes or more, and in that time, I gradually felt at ease, feeling strangely happy within.

The light vanished and I fell into a deep sleep. For the next few months I thought about what had happened, to find the answers. I went to a spiritual church, but it was five months after I saw the light. After asking different people about the light. orange meant an inner cleansing of one's self, it also is one of the healing colours. The first visit to the church was to leave me with wonderful memories of my father, who passed over some eight years before. The medium at the service gave me a reading concerning my father and I, when he was on the earth plane. I was the only person who could understand what he was saying, even my own family would not have understood. It made me cry, most of what was said was personal to me.

But one part I will share with you. My father was ill for a very long time. He passed over in hospital. He suffered from advanced senility but passed over with lung cancer. I had been thinking to myself since my father's passing, that I was beginning to have some memory loss and for this reason I thought I might develop it. My thoughts on this subject were picked up by spirit and relayed back to my father through the medium, he told me I would not get it, the bad memory in my case was caused by over-work. Another interesting thing he said was that when he was in hospital and family and friends came to see him, whatever was said to him or about him, he could fully understand but could not make his body work to make them understand. With this illness my father could not speak. Doctors may not agree with this, but spirit never lie. I have learnt since becoming spiritual, to never underestimate the power and knowledge of spirit. There is in spirit a vast reservoir of knowledge, waiting to be tapped, when attuned to spirit trained or self taught the sky's the limit. I've often had dreams of helping people through healing, long before I became spiritual. All people have dreams some come true, I am now a qualified practising healer.

Communication Part One

Feeling touch intuition = awareness. Friends and family who have passed over, communicate by touching me, or by using the power of telepathy. Which is the transfer of thought from one dimension to the other, from your mind to theirs. Normally when my family are around me, they touch the side of my head with their fingers, pressing lightly nearly always on the right hand side. Sometimes when I'm driving my van and danger's near and I can't see it they press my head firmly, my reaction to this is to slow down. within one mile there is always trouble. either an accident or some other obstruction in the road. I started to get these warnings shortly after I had a bad accident. I was travelling at 45mph along a dry road, when the car in front of me suddenly stopped, at the same time indicating to turn left, but failed to do so. I slid towards the rear of the car, there were two children in the back with their pet dog, mum and dad in the front seat. As there were cars coming in the opposite direction, I had to make a split second decision, I chose to go for the kerb, expecting to hit the kerb but I did not hit it dead on, instead I hit it side wheel on, I bounced through the air, 180 degree turn and came down on my side. I was not wearing a seat belt.If I had been wearing it, I'm sure it would have killed me.

Communication Part Two

When I first started to communicate with spirit, I felt that I was asking and answering my own questions. It soon became apparent that I was not, all the answers back were unexpected and always logical. The very first time I tried it I relaxed myself completely took all daily thoughts from my mind and asked if there were any spirits there, to my amazement I had spirit faces staring at me in full colour, some with blue eyes some with brown, people that I've never met before. As the learning process continues you begin to talk to your guides my nearest guide is a Red Indian called Little Bear, he is of the Blackfoot tribe. When I talk to my guides I always refer to them as friends, and call them by their names, they always call me by my name. On learning about a guide, I ask them their name, their nationality and all general things about them.

My next friend is my healer he too is a Red Indian, his name is Silver Fox, his tribe is Shoshuni. He is called a Shaman or powerful medicine man. Each guide is on a different level of spirit, some are contacted by a deeper meditation, on the next level my friend Tei Lei (pronounced Tay Lay) is a man of great wisdom, he gives me most of my thoughts (not the rude ones). My next friend was given to me first by a medium in the early stages of learning, his name is Tegjet he is Egyptian. He was on the earth plane an architect, responsible for the foundations of the pyramids at Giza, also for the carving of the Sphinx. The date he gave me was 8,500 BC.

From what I can gather from reading some books, is that geologists do not agree with this date, I would not argue with them, I accept what they tell me from spirit. Thought is the most powerful energy there is and used in the right way can heal a person you have never seen, who might live on the other side of the world. If all people had spiritual knowledge, there might not be any wars again, people could always live in peace. healing can never be guaranteed but many miracles happen. Many diseases can and are cured by spiritual healing, one of the best healers in England was Harry Edwards, and his books make good reading. Anyone reading this book and requiring healing can go to any spiritual church and ask for it, or you can telephone the Harry Edwards Healing Sanctuary at Burrows Lea, Shere, Nr Guildford, Surrey. They will give you absent healing. I give absent healing every day. I meet people in my daily work who need help, or they know someone who does. It normally comes out in general conversation, very often I don't tell them. healing energies can help all living things.

Auras and Lights

Auras surround all people, these I'm told are different colours white and gold. I personally cannot see the light energies with my open eyes. But I've been told that I've got the colour orange around me. orange is one of the healing colours, others being blue and purple. When in the circle I often got the colour green I was asked by the medium what I thought it meant, my answer to this was that it means the beginning of all life on this planet, take green out of the planet and we all perish. Simply meaning new spiritual life.

Clairvoyance

The power of seeing things that others cannot , or sometimes called second sight.

Mediums

To give messages from the spirit dimension

Trance Mediums

A trance medium is a person who is taken over by spirit, the spirit speaks through the medium, normally their own guide.

For myself, as a healer I have to be a medium, to be able to tune into spirit to pass the healing energies to the patient. I can also see spirit sometimes, normally in churches. They are on occasions very clear. In 1993 I went to Midnight Mass at our local church, it was my intention to speak to the lady vicar that weekend, during the service a spirit woman came in through the ceiling, and came very close to the vicar, she was an attractive lady in her fifties I thought. She had a long polka dot dress and a blouse that was done up to the top of the neck, with a frill at the top. Her hair was done up high with a bun, her hair was dark brown, brown eyes and a bent nose.

14

When I spoke to the vicar I told her what I had seen, she left the room and returned with a photograph of the woman exactly as I described her.

Another friend of mine once asked me to tune into spirit at an agreed time, she was to get a message for me, and I for her. After closing my eyes I tuned in, after a short time I asked if anyone was there, the answer came from a very young boy. He told me to get pen and paper ready, he then said write this down - Perambulator, baby boy, blond hair, blue eyes, Rachael, Sean/Sam. I then asked if there was any more information, he answered no that's your lot goodbye. When I gave my friend the message she could not take it, I said to her that Rachael was pregnant, Rachael being her daughter, she said she wasn't, I thought will wait and see. Two weeks later her daughter who then was living in Dorset, telephoned her mother and told her she was pregnant, and was coming home. Spirit knew before Rachael, I told Rachael what had happened, she said that she also thought she was going to have a boy. She gave birth to a lovely baby boy with blond hair and blue eyes. The only thing wrong was the name, although her mother mentioned the name Sean to her and made a point of saying that it meant God's little gift.

Regression/Past Lives.

Before I became spiritual I went to see a hypnotist and asked her if she would regress me. I had always felt that my last life had a bearing on this one. I was wrong. On two visits to see her I was able to go back four lives, on the first occasion I went back to 1520. I was in this life a surf working with a woodsman on a large estate in Nottinghamshire, at the point I was regressed to, the first sounds from myself were laughter, the woodsman that I was working with had fallen over a log and into a bog. In this picture I could see a woman on a horse, she too was laughing. My age at the time was sixteen, I was asked by the hypnotist what I was wearing and I described the shoes and clothes I had on. If I had given the wrong answer to this it would have proved that it had not worked. The disappointing thing about this regression was that she didn't ask enough questions. I was then taken forward to my next life, at the point of entry to this life I found myself in great pain, I had just been run through with a sword. In this life the year was 1651, the battle of Worcester. I was a royalist, this was the last battle of the second uprising. My name in this life was Robert Laurent. I was married and my age was 29.

On my second visit I returned to the year 1750 my age was 56 and I passed over at 64. I was in this life an aristocrat, at the point of entry I was warming my bottom by the fire. My name was Robert Lacey I was looking after my brother's estate in Surrey, his name was George. After being taken forward towards my next life, when asked where I was I said I was in spirit,

15

I was sitting in a garden talking to my friends. I was then taken forward again, at the point of entry the year was 1876 and 36 years old. I was a manager of a printing company, and I was standing on a pavement in the City of London it was my break period. The company I worked for was called Bates and sons, but I've never checked this out. In 1876 there were horse-drawn trams, I could see them everywhere, carriages and carts. When asked I told the hypnotist the address where I lived I gave as 22 Green Lanes Enfield, and that I was married with three children. Thomas was 10 Emily 12 and Ellen 14. My wife's name was Lillian, the hypnotist brought me forward to my life's end. It was to be the most emotional experience I've ever had. The year was 1902 I was lying in my bed, waiting to pass over, in great pain, a tightness in my chest, my wife and children and their children were gathered around the bed. I had consumption, I started to cry at this point, the hypnotist took me forward quickly. Asked then where I was and I replied in spirit, this was my last life I was born in this life in 1945. I cannot forget the closing of my last life it will remain with me for the rest of this one. As this was my last life everything was much clearer and more precise. My name in that life was Stephen Royce.

Chapter 2 : Sayings

The Love of Money is the Route of all Evil

One of my father's favourite sayings, and so very true, the lack of it and the greed of it. It affects people within, changes their outlook on life, the poor people are sometimes envious of the rich and dream of becoming lottery millionaires, and then say it won't change my life. There is nothing wrong in earned wealth, providing you're not grossly overpaid. People who inherit wealth are often out of touch with reality. I'm not trying to be political here merely passing on spiritual thinking. Some people make their money out of the misery of others, by bad working conditions, long hours of work, by intimidation the threat of losing one's job, if you speak out. Wealthy people have so much to learn, some of course are very charitable. At the same time some like the media's attention when they make a kind gesture. I would say look after your staff, before your shareholders dividend. If your business is around live animals do not make money and be cruel to them. Make money yes but let your animals have some dignity. For poor people, most of you are probably content with your lot, but for some of you will be looking for that pot of gold at the end of the rainbow. If you want to get there be honest about it, dishonesty only brings self inflicted misery. That's spirit advice, take it or leave it.

Food for Thought

Most of my writing is concerned with the welfare of animals. Their mistreatment for the sake of money or lust. Animals in my opinion do not as a rule get enough thought, true there are many charities doing excellent work. But people who care about the overall concept of animals are in the minority. Spiritual thinking has allowed me to understand that the spiritual level of animals are on a higher level than ours, for the reasons stated above. Spiritual thinking is for all creatures, not just us.

Lambs to the Slaughter

My understanding is that English farmers get more money for live animals than dead ones, so for this reason the animals are herded into lorries and shipped to the continent. With no consideration for the animal. 'Hooray' in 1994/1995 people are beginning to wake up and protest about this and hopefully bring about the end to this cruelty. What spirit would like to ask you is to have a better understanding of life, think before you make a decision that will affect the outcome of a person or animal's life, think for them as well as yourself, place people's and animal's lives before profit. When you can overcome greed, you can overcome anything, and start to become a person again.

If the Cap Fits, Wear it

Every day in our green and pleasant land, we are reading in our newspapers about the royal family, some good and some bad. As their subjects we know that they are supposed to set us an example, but they are failing to do so. Almost it seems, every week they are showing themselves up. Apart from their unearned wealth, they are no different from us. Like the church they are large land keepers. Land and material things are owned by no one in this world you are only the keepers of during your lifetime, you can't take it with you. One of the worst examples of the royal family and also some of the rich, is this lust for death in our countryside. Taking young children on hunts, to kill the beautiful fox, or if they are lucky kill a huge ferocious hare. To tear from limb to limb, watched over in amusement by their elders.

On a bad day the pack might even trespass on to someone's property and kill their pet dog or cat. Big brave men and women and children looking on, happy at seeing so much despair. In this lifetime they will learn the difference between right and wrong, but they won't let on. Some royal's however are truly spiritual people, with the kind gestures they make towards people for example those suffering with AIDS (in this country they are sometimes treated like lepers) and others visit old people's homes and hospices, but these dear souls are in the minority, as far as royal's go. Have you ever noticed how many animal charities they are patrons of, where's the example there, they kill too much wildlife and spirit have strong feelings about it. The royal's who help others are the ones who have voiced their opinions against killing wildlife. (This speaks volumes does it not). Things about some people need to be said, we cannot stand by and watch it happen, we have to cry stop sooner or later. It's unfortunate that they feel its their divine right to do as they please, it's not. They have to set an example to the rest of us. They also should not be allowed to override the law either, what's good for one is good for the rest, they are not a law unto themselves, we must find a happy solution to this problem. When they pray, do they ask for the next Derby winner, or do they reflect and think what lucky people they are. They are even going to have oil wells now. All of us can be criticised by others, but the royal's are in the public eye. I do not envy them, I pity them, because some of them have lost sight of reality. Spirit will continue to be near them, and try to influence them, where they can. I often feel that if I could talk to them, I might be able to improve their lives. The royal's have had much written about them, some justified and some not. I wish them no ill will and that they learn from their mistakes.

As I write this book, I often feel that I've exhausted all thoughts and then all of a sudden I'm off again. Spirit say we will tell you, when we are finished.

What You Never Have You Never Miss

India should be, but isn't a classless society. There are thousands of have's and millions of have-nots. But in the case of India, the have-nots are very lucky people. They have a way about them that shames the West. No one man will be richer than his neighbour. In their communities, they look after one another. In the eye of the West, they all live in extreme poverty. Two years ago in 1993, I was lucky enough to go on holiday, touring the northern part of India, the famous triangle of Delhi, Agra, and Jaipur, I met all different sorts of people, from all walks of life. Apart from a few exceptions, most of the people were not greedy, like people in the West. They worked hard to earn what rupees they could, in happiness from what I could see. To earn a little money from the tourists, they would always offer them a small service. One day while visiting a mosque, men were cutting the grass with this huge lawn mower, that is normally pushed, but they had it harnessed to a sacred cow, it was comical to watch. They would ask tourists if they wanted to take photographs, for that they would get a small reward. I also met there and saw for the first time in my life, lepers who would gladly shake your hand, I found them cheerful and very pleased to meet you. One such man I met in Jaipur, he was standing in the road on crutches, he had only half fingers and thumbs on each hand, and one foot had withered away. He was one of the most happy men I met in India. We talked briefly, he could speak good English, I gladly offered him some money. I found that most of the beggars in India were either lepers or people with terrible diseases and the only able bodied beggars are what the Indians call gypsies, who all came from Bangladesh.

I met this young boy in Agra outside the Red Fort, on a bridge and he was begging. He was about ten years' old he spoke to me and I offered him some money, I then walked on, he called out goodbye, and I turned round to acknowledge him and saw the whole of him. He was suffering from Elephantitis, his feet were about 18 inches long, 10 inches wide and 5 inches thick, with only two toes on each foot, he walked on the side of his feet. The sight made me weep, but he was laughing, he made me feel humble. I will never forget him, or any of the lepers I met. A lesson was learnt from this experience. I will be going back to India when funds allow, their way of life is good to see, and be amongst, they are spiritual people, but may not know it. One of the people in our party gave the children Biro pens, you would think they were gold bars, their faces lit up, they were a pleasure to watch. So for what I've seen in different countries, the poorer you are the happier you are. What you never have you never miss.

Let He Who Is Without Sin Cast The First Stone

Jesus said these words and how right he was. There are plenty of people in this world, who judge and make accusations about other people, without taking into account their own lives. There is not a person living on this planet who has not done anything wrong. Be careful about your assumptions, don't set yourself up to be a laughing stock.

Easier Said Than Done

How many times do people say things that they will do, but never carry out. Politicians say many things in their manifesto's but do so many u-turns they become giddy. How many of us say when we meet friends and relatives, that we will come and visit you soon or you say we will invite you round soon but never do. A change of attitudes is required here, be positive, say we will see you soon and mean it. Politicians say what you mean truth-fully, so that we all understand.

What You Sow You Reap

In one way or another this saying applies to all of us. For example if you do not bring your children up correctly, they very often go off the rails, bringing you nothing but grief. This saying applies to good things as well as bad. If you brought your child up to show respect for others and in a loving environment, the child will grow normally, into a dependable person all their lives. Or for instance, if you were offered an item that had fallen off the back of a lorry, for we'll say £20, you will almost certainly find that sooner or later something unexpectedly will go wrong and end up costing you £40. Best to be honest in the first place. Your initial gain is someone else's loss.

Chapter 3: Guides and Teachers

Tejget

This is an update on deeper conversations with Tejget. I have been following the article in the Daily Mail about the Sphinx and pyramids at Giza. They now believe the Sphinx was carved 10,000 years ago. I tuned into my friend Tejget to ask him for more information, regarding his work with the pyramids. He agreed with the findings, stating that 5,500 years ago his people were the last survivors of a highly intelligent race of people. They in fact laid the foundations as he said before for the pyramids. But it was the Athenians who built them and not the Egyptians. So my first assumption that Tejget was an Egyptian was wrong. He told me that the pyramids were not intended to be burial chambers, but were intended to be places of healing. Each pyramid of different size was to heal different things. The alignment to the stars is correct it was his people who were responsible for this. This will be explained in a minute.

His people were as I've already said far more technically and spiritually advanced than people today. He told me that his people were called Athenians and came from the area we used to call Persia. They first came to Persia 20,000 years ago. The Athenians were the people who carved the original Sphinx, it was carved as half man and half beast. A man's head and body and feet of a beast. The carving was to illustrate the closeness of spiritual understanding between man and animal. The great pyramid was to be where the strongest power of healing could be had, As with whats known the points of the pyramids were to be in direct line with Orion. The three planets that they pointed to were where the Athenians came from originally, the smallest planet and the one that's slightly off centre is called Ramoss, the centre one is called Zeeda and the next one Acille, that being the English pronunciation of their names.

The healing energies would have worked like this, the pyramids were to be totally empty inside, the energies would be transmitted from the planet in line to the top of the pyramid. The energies would then have dispersed to the lower levels. If a person was seeking healing he or she would sit on the floor with backs to the wall, help would be asked for through meditation, the great pyramid was the place for the strongest healing as the power was so strong you could be suffering with almost anything and be sure of a cure. This race of people suffered not too many illnesses as they were very close to the energy source. They were to be built for all mankind regardless of race or creed.

Chapter 4: Brains

Paranormal

As a spiritual thinker the word paranormal for me does not exist. Because with the knowledge comes insight, into things not everybody understands, for example UFO's and other life force on other planets. In tuning into spirit I have asked questions about other planets and peoples. I once asked, from where did Earth man come from the answer back was exact and fast, from the planet Mirranda. I cannot prove this but spirit never lie. When this conversation first started and I was talking about UFO's and other peoples, I was told who was I to think that earth people were the only people, that put me in my place. Paranormal is always used to describe what's not understood. Television programmes always use this word.

There are many planets where other peoples live, it would account for the many sightings in our skies of UFO's, these sightings cannot be ignored. It amazes me why so many are hushed up, these people are far more advanced than us, and have learnt not to be war like. I'm told that they are compassionate people and mean us no harm as they are light years ahead of us, their thinking and actions are completely different to ours. In this lifetime I hope to be able to communicate with them using the power of telepathy, when spiritual thought is understood these sightings and the possible meeting of these will be accepted. During the many conversations that I've had with spirit on this subject, I once said to them that I felt that their form of travel was powered by thought I felt it would account for the very fast speeds they travel at. The answer back to this question was, that I was thinking along the right lines, but was not quite there yet. I will get there in the end.

Psychologists

A person who studies the human mind, these people who study this subject study hard for most of their lives, to learn from teachers and books that really have limited knowledge on the subject. They may know more than I do about the workings of the brain. But unfortunately most people think that the mind is in the brain, but I'm afraid it's not. The complexities of the brain will puzzle most people for always, the mind however, the understanding of it and how it works is within everybody's capabilities. Psychologists are often on television shows relating to the so-called paranormal (I dislike that word), they are the ones who always give a negative reaction to anything spiritual, forming opinions from their limited knowledge on the subject. Unfortunately they have become typecast, as soon as they open their mouths to speak out comes the same answer. They all seem to be like preprogrammed robots. I do not of course wish to sound unfeeling towards these people, but I do wish that they would learn about spiritual matters, before they speak about what they know nothing about. I always feel quite sorry for them, there is one woman psychologist that often appears on the television and I do feel sorry for her. If I was able to speak to her I might be able to help her, I will not mention her name in case I offend her.

Psychologists will always have work to do and I and spirit know that they also can and do help many people. The way forward is greater spiritual understanding, where every human being can benefit from the knowledge. None of you will have to pass exams for this knowledge, even if you cannot read or write you can still receive the spiritual knowledge. All the problems of this planet can be answered without ever going to school, this will come about in the distant future. But schools of one kind or another in spirit and on the earth plane, can still teach discipline, how to behave and to show respect for others. In the future when thinking changes there will be no need of prisons, no need of law and order, with the change of thinking comes the realisation that all life is a simple process. One very important factor is that we never actually lose consciousness from one life to the next, we will all instinctively know what to do and this includes all animals. The one very important thing that bonds all life on this planet earth together is love. That one emotion holds this planet together in unison with the spiritual dimension. So my psychologist friends do not ever underestimate anything spiritual. The answers you always seem to give fall flat, we think that most of you in part do understand but you seem to hold yourselves back.

Zodiac Signs

A lot of people run their lives on the Zodiac signs. They have to be right for someone. But your life and destiny was chosen by you, when you were last in spirit. Your spiritual pathway is your destiny, you will never be able to deviate from this pathway, you can try to alter things as much as you like, you will fail. I am a strong willed person and I always try to achieve my goal. Generosity hard work and honesty all go to make a good Leo. Even I look at the stars and Patrick Walker is my favourite astrologer. Spiritual thinking is beyond astrology so I look at the signs for a bit of fun. Though it would be true to say that according to the signs Piscean women are a bad match for Leo and I would agree with that. My wife's another strong willed Leo and so is our son, my wife and I often clash. So it would seem, that there's a lot of truth in them. Patrick Walker is now in spirit.

Chapter 5: Sayings

Before the Cows Come Home

For all the people who had read this book, especially the ones who are well educated and perhaps have scientific minds, no doubt many of you will have frowned on some of the things you have read. Please remember this, all the information that I have received has come from the spiritual dimension. You will have to accept that there are people in spirit with a far higher knowledge than you and that they will have for ever more. All the knowledge that I have received has only touched the edge of what's available. I must consider myself very lucky indeed, to have been able to communicate through telepathic means. The communication will continue all my life with them, and when I pass this life I will be reunited with them again. So before the cows come home try to broaden your horizons, try to understand where some of your own intelligence comes from. We can take on through our fathers genes some of the good and the bad, but the spirit within us is pure. Your spirit contains your mind, where information is passed on to you by your spirit guides so that you can work on it to formulate ideas and work out your own conclusions.

All the relevant details of your life are stored in your mind and when you pass this life, it will be recalled by spirit. If you are however a skeptical person your day will come sooner or later, and proof will be there for all to see. It is not possible to argue against anything spiritual because the skeptics are the very ones who have no knowledge at all. I feel very sorry for those people who walk about with blinkers on, all their lives. How many times have you heard someone say or perhaps said yourself, that I've been here before, well you have. I often listen to arguments on the television from skeptics who try to explain why they don't believe in whatever or try from their own educated mind to give an answer to something spiritual, it holds no water for me. I wish that sometimes I could talk to these people, I know that I could help them. To be skeptical is to be negative in thinking. Skeptics miss so much of the good things in life, you probably do not agree and your values are very different to mine. For the people who have enjoyed reading this book the sky's the limit for you. It has given me enormous pleasure in writing it, I have been able to receive so much knowledge unknown to man today, will I ever write another? I do not know.

As Sure as Eggs are Eggs

Life on the earth as we know it will inevitably change. As each century passes, the spirituality of man will change for the better. The earth and its resources will be used to the benefit of all mankind, and not the usual minority who make vast fortunes from exploiting our planet. In the future all this will change, there will come a time when power energy will be free, it will come about by new advanced technology of a kind not known to man today. We will by then be different thinkers and this new technology will be passed to us by our Mirrandian ancestors. In fact most of our future learning will come from other worlds, by using our telepathic abilities. We will be be able to keep in contact with our families who have passed over, you will be able to communicate with them, like you did when they were on the earth plane, until their life in spirit comes to an end and they return to the earth plane with a new family. Our life expectancy will increase with advanced technology, we will in time live the long lives, as they do on other planets, in time to come the average age of man will be 250 years.

The world will become more free of diseases, with the change of thinking comes more rational behaviour. The birth rate in over populated areas will fall at a tremendous rate. All people will become more sensible, there will be no need for money and we will have a one class society. With this change of thinking comes a change of our now war like nature, there will be no more wars and all conflict will end. By this time we will have learnt new ways of producing our food, self created from our own energy. Space travel will be the norm, not travelling like today, when in earth time its calculated, as for example 50 light years from a-b, it will eventually take only seconds. A statement that will make most of you frown, but nevertheless this will happen in the future. The shame is that at about 12,000 years ago the earth already had this technology.

As the Athenians died out and why they did I'm not quite sure, the technology died with them, perhaps they went home. Only by more communication could I find out. But my teachers have told me that all future knowledge that I receive now will be of the present and the future. I must go forward with my learning, I still have to learn about the thought levels five-nine at the moment it feels mind boggling to me. With the knowledge of the levels will come more information on other planets, there is so much to learn, I hope I live long enough, so as the title of this chapter says, as sure as eggs are eggs all these changes will happen.

To Be Or Not To Be

I am at the moment reading a book about Mother Teresa and her army of helpers, the book is as much as I expected. I have mentioned earlier in this book about Mother Teresa and I will be repeating some of what's already been said. I will say this that spirit think very highly of her, because of the work she has done and is doing all over the earth, all this work is spiritual and her as well as the others are all carrying out their spiritual lessons. The only difference between her understanding and mine is, is that she believes in God and isn't knowing. She is Roman Catholic and religious, there is nothing wrong with that, except that through my knowledge I know that Christ has lived many lives since the crucifixion. As has his family and most of the people you read about in the Bible. What Christ stood for is very important and I like so many others look to his ways for guidance.

Christ is not God, He spoke of His Father in heaven, the Father is the God, but not a man, God or white light is pure thinking energy with a power source you could never imagine.

If in between lives we could get to level nine we would have the answer, I do not think that spirit will give me this knowledge, I have not asked them about it, it's just a feeling I have. Mother Teresa will understand what's written here, she will not be offended. I think that she is truly the most spiritual woman living on this earth, it's only names and understanding that's different between us. It's her spirit guides who tell her what she needs to know. When her time comes to leave the earth plane and to go home, she will remain in spirit on level two or three, she will carry on her healing there. From the spiritual dimension she is seen as a bright light, shining bright in the dark. Mother Teresa you have set an example that all churches should follow, discarding their fine robes and mitres and their fine living. Peter should work for the people with the people, healing the people. In a time to come churches and religions as we know them today will disappear forever, they will be replaced with new thinking, a greater spiritual understanding will fall upon us, and we will become whole again.

The Best Thing Since Sliced Bread

The above saying might be used by persons who are describing another person of the opposite sex. Many people choose their partners for the way they look. Muscular body in a man perhaps, or an attractive curving figure in a woman. But what are these people really like, do outwardly attractive people have kind hearts, are they underneath their skin cruel or aggressive in their ways. You cannot see these things when you are smitten by the way people look. The best way to select a partner is to look within whoever you fancy. Find out from others in the first instance, their friends maybe to what they are really like. Are they quick-tempered, could they be aggressive towards you. You will not see the traits in a person you've been drawn to because of their good looks. Do not be put off by someone you might consider ugly. Because underneath their exterior you will often find a very caring person. When looking for your opposite number look within, for this is where the true beauty of a person dwells.

A Problem Shared is a Problem Halved

Every person on this earth without exception has had at one time or another problems. These problems are varied and most of us keep the more serious ones to ourselves. Secrets stored away forever, and from time to time removed from our minds store-room and remembered. If all of us were to share these problems with trusted friends or family, then the problems would be halved. When you finally buck up courage to admit something and perhaps hold a discussion on it, you will probably find that in most cases that the problem wasn't really there.

Not For All The Tea In China

Not until your purpose in this life has been fulfiled, will you leave the earth plane for spirit. You will remain on the earth plane until all the tasks that have been set for you are completed, no matter what age you live to. As you know you can pass at all ages, from aborted babies to the very few who live past 100 years, and there is nothing you can do about it either, money will not help you in any way. This is worth a mention, for all those people who waste their money on having their remains frozen after death, in case in some distant future a cure could be found for them, 'forget it', there is no life without spirit. When you die in this life your spirit passes onto the next, it will not be coming back into your present body. By the time the cure is found your spirit will more than likely have found a new life on the earth plane, once the spirit has left the body it will only return if its immediately (out of body experiences happen at this time). The only exception to the rule is, when a person is in a long coma, if the person is to return to full working order the spirit will return. So all the tea in China will not change your fate. Anyway when you realise how wonderful it is in spirit, you will not want to come back anyway.

Don't Do As I Do, Do As I Say.

This saying could apply to any one of us, for this chapter I will refer all of it to our government. Being for most of them the decent Christian souls they think they are, spirit will say this, they have informed all working people in England, that we must keep our wage demands in line with inflation. This is an example of what actually takes place. Nurses 2% hospital management 7% and the government double pay. Does it not seem strange that the very people who have so much less are never given more and the well-off get the most. This kind of issue breeds contempt from the less well off, encourages crime and can create rebellious thinking. Most of us are poor, we have to pay heavy taxes to pay the greedy. For instance, former nationalised industries after being privatised, the poor have to pay a lot more in charges, but their directors or better known (fat cats receive huge salaries at our expense. How is this financial self worth assessed? How do these greedy people sleep at nights? Do they go to church every Sunday assuming that they are Christian? Who says that you are worthy of these unfair rises? Can you sleep at night and be content within? or do you actually consider the less well off. All of you are known by spirit the ones who care and the ones who don't, whether you are Christian or not. But for most of our government they are just plain greedy, poor representatives of our communities.

How many of you are there who can proudly stand up and say I'm not interested in money or what it brings, I'm only interested in the people I serve and that I'm very aware of the people's plight, one or two maybe. It's only too easy for someone like myself to criticise this government, but my personal feelings on this have not come into it, all that's written here has come direct from spirit, they prefer to talk about the good things on the earth and how we can accomplish more, they do not like offending anyone, but sometimes things have to be said, and most of us don't like hearing it. The government of today or tomorrow should be looking at the welfare of all and understand that life does not revolve around money alone. Instead of the people's money feeding bottomless pits, we should spend more on the sick and the disabled and on re-educating our young to higher standards, and to actually bring about a one class society (which is what it is in spirit). The one class society will only come about with a change of thinking. How can the leaders of our government talk about a one class society when some of their members are super rich it seems to spirit that these are false words. It does not matter who is in government you all have so much to learn. This chapter could so easily have been written from my own heart, but I must not judge you, but spirit will.

Blood is Thicker Than Water

His name was Charles, he lived a part of his life an extremely lonely man. No one, including his neighbours and the DHSS cared about him or for him. An elderly once proud man left to fend for himself, living out his life in a dingy flat, his only known family his son living in America. Charles was burgled many times, and they took what little money he had, one day among other things they stole his pension book, Charles reported his loss to the DHSS who in turn lent him the measly sum of £31 to buy some food. He was told by the DHSS that he must repay the loan, but he was never able to do so, so the DHSS never replaced his stolen pension book. His neighbours called the police because there was an awful smell coming from his flat, when they found Charles he lay on the floor and his old body was decomposing. His neighbours said that he was a misery and hard to get along with, well wouldn't you be? Left alone to fend for yourself, with apart from your four walls no one to talk to, day in and day out, and then to add insult to injury left to starve to death because of having no money to buy food with. Isn't it a sad reflection on today's society in allowing this to happen. He resides in spirit now, back home with his mum and dad, surrounded in love and looking back to his life on the earth, with total disbelief.

Chapter 6: Heaven Sent

Rich Man Poor Man

Wealth today is seen as the gathering of material possessions all the things you cannot take with you. With wealth comes greed and envy and bad feeling between people, you can however be the poor man and you can still be rich. Wealth for myself comes from my spiritual knowledge, once grasped you quickly forget the need for material wealth. I'll not deny that we all have to live in some form of shelter and most of us have to have transport. The rich man who makes his money on the backs of others causing misery or cheating and stealing, will have a lot to answer for, when passed over. He or she's lesson will have to be learnt.

Lives Saved Lessons Learnt

Apart from passing over from old age, people's lives that are saved from accidents or the like are meant for higher things. Sometime in their lives they will probably do a kind deed for someone or care for someone else who's ill. People who help others freely, will have a higher spiritual level while on the Earth plane and they will take it with them on passing. As you live each life you will progress by learning lessons, it might be a lesson on tolerance poverty, wealth, being criminal. If you are, for example, a criminal then you have negative thinking and your spirit level will be lower, if however you are kind in thought as well as deed then you are positive and on a higher level. When returning to spirit lessons learnt go with you. Positive thinking always results in good things as negative is the opposite. If you can't be compassionate, you can't be your spiritual self, caring people are light years ahead of the others.

Passing Over

Just a few lines to say, when your time comes and leading up to it please don't worry about it, it's just like stepping off the kerb. In time to come death will be a time of joy rather than sorrow, when spirit is better understood. In time to come loved ones will be able to contact you, grief will become a thing of the past. Of course most of you will not be able to accept this and I fully understand.

In Time to Come

If a third of this planet's population were like minded spiritually, together they could do so much good. To change the minds of nations at war, and create a lasting peace, to stop the innocent creatures and trees from destruction in the rain forests and elsewhere, to stop the barbaric killing of the whales for all time. All these things can be done and will be done in time to come, good will destroy evil, but not in this lifetime. If you are a penniless person, maybe a down and out, but you give of yourself, God's light will shine on you forever. I personally do not look at any man or woman, be they tramp or millionaire any the less, they all have spiritual wealth if they look for it. All men and women are equal poor or rich.

'Oh When, Oh When'

More people today seem to be aware of animals suffering, animals have always suffered from exploitation. How man treats animals leaves a lot to be desired, it's one thing to kill for food, but for the blood lust thugs who kill for pleasure, or in the name of sport, these people are on a lower spiritual level than the very animals they kill. Falling into this category for example, hunting and the killing of the beautiful fox the brown bear in the forests of Rumania, and the unforgivable killing of the gentle whales. Nature always takes care of it's own, corrects its own balance. As a spiritual person I have to forgive these people, its very hard. 'Oh When Oh When' is it going to stop.

This also applies to the rearing of farm animals, although many farmers are caring people, I would ask you not to put profit before welfare. Why can't the hunting fraternity hunt people instead, just for fun, why can't more nations have more cruise ships to visit and watch the whales, they could do the same for the Bears in Rumania, most people would rather see them alive than dead. The country would earn much more revenue. I feel that animals are on a higher level than us, they do not for example commit murder or take drugs. They do stay loyal to their families, their young ones are brought up with strict control. The people of this planet could do their learning by watching animals, if they could follow their example, the world would be a far happier place.

Mothers Little Ones.

For the many mothers in this world of ours, can you imagine the uproar if it was the general rule, to take your babies away from you, the hurt and pain this would cause. Additional food for thought, why do people (farmers in this case) take young calves away from their mothers, normally only a few days old, imagine the pain this causes to both the mother and calf, I've even heard recently on the radio, the cows feel nothing when they are taken away, what utter rubbish. The reason for this is of course money, to send the unfortunate ones abroad for fattening for veal in crates. To be spiritual you feel their pain, we see on the television the way they are kept in their crates waiting to die a few weeks later. It's enough to make you vegetarian isn't it. I would personally never eat veal, because I know the suffering it causes. All creatures should be allowed to pass over with dignity.

Someone Somewhere

Why do we treat our planet with so much disrespect, the worlds climate has started to change, mainly out of ignorance of the western nations. Who don't seem to care, when it comes to industry polluting our rivers, the sea, and destroying the ozone layer. All governments do little about it, they waffle on, all talk and no action. It all boils down to money and nothing else. Governments look after the big industrialists, not wishing to offend them, in case they don't fill their coffers, with funds for party support. The worlds population are going to learn a bitter lesson with this getting out of hand. If you are not worried about your present life, then think about your grandchildren's lives. What hell on earth life are they going to have.

Governments the world over have got to get off their behinds and do something collectedly about it. Fine offending companies millions of pounds or dollars every time they cause pollution. Then use this money to put things right. For every gallon of chemical emptied into our rivers, fine them, even if it puts them out of business. Someone somewhere has to take responsibility. This beautiful planet, slowly being destroyed, because of pollution, animals can't tell us, they have to rely on us and spirit to do something about it. Telling off and small fines for polluters is not good enough, a sharp lesson has to be learnt. All the way along the scale, from animal cruelty to the industrial polluter, all countries of this planet are guilty of one thing or another. Whether they allow oil pipes to continue to spill onto the land, rivers and sea, because they won't repair them. Or the destruction of the rain forests and the animals within.

For God's sake wake up. These words need to be said, I'm the spokesman for spirit, I don't usually mix my words. Spirit know that there are millions of people on this planet who care about what's written here. Spirit will always be near the ones who care. You can all see what can be done, when some of our rivers have been cleared of pollution, and wildlife return to them. Now something else, in meditation spirit have told me, that in time the world will turn a full circle and through learning, the planet will return to how it used to be. Hopefully without cars and motorways hopefully with people being kind to one another and no drugs, murder, wars or money, back to the days of bartering maybe.

Goodness Gracious Me

When I first wrote these words above, I was stumped for what to write about them. One February evening in 1995 I was out walking my dogs Rolo and Amy, both Cocker Spaniel's. When thoughts came flooding into my head, spirit wanted me to write about more of my own experiences, relating to the connection between spirit and myself. I've had my small business for nearly twelve years and through the recession have had difficult times. I'm not normally the type of person who would ask anyone else for help, apart from my bank, which falls on deaf ears. They only seem to

31

want to help you when the climate is rosy, and they fall over themselves trying to lend you money. However, when the recession came attitudes changed, bringing about a hardness.

My bank is no different than any other when times are hard. They seem to stop being people with a non-caring attitude. In late spring of 1994. I asked spirit if they could help me, I wasn't looking for a pools win or any financial reward, just help in solving my business worries. Before I tell you what happened, I have to say, that spirit will always help people who help spirit. For example healing, caring, being compassionate. Three days after asking, a strange thing happened, one of my customers who to my knowledge has never offered help in any way, and why should he you might be thinking. With all my customers rightly or wrongly I've always formed a close relationship with. Calling them my friends even if the feelings not mutual, listen to their problems and sometimes they listen to mine. It's them and their families I've got to know over the years.

So getting back to what happened. This customer told me that he had recommended me to another company, that was in the process of closing down. When speaking to the owner he recommended me to some of his most reliable customers. I quickly telephoned them all, and was lucky enough to supply five shops. Which at that time saved my bacon. So you see spirit can work wonders when you need them. Goodness gracious me.

Going Against the Grain

Like in sawing wood against the grain, life can be troublesome. Have you ever noticed while out walking or driving the car, the looks on some people's faces. Stone-faced I sometimes think, not to be unfair, most of us at one time or another look like this. But it seems that more and more people today are looking this way. Sometimes when walking my dogs and I meet other people I normally acknowledge them by saying good morning or good evening and give them a smile, it melts their expression and they smile back in appreciation. The moral of this story is to smile a lot, and help take the gloom out of life.

To all Intents and Purposes

In 1992 in August, I was visiting my wife in hospital, she was recovering from an eye operation. The woman in the next bed had been totally blind all her life. She was given the chance of sight in one eye, by having a cornea transplant. She told me that this was the third time she had had a transplant and that the previous two had failed, also that she had the operation ten days earlier and was still blind. As she was a smoker, she would often make her way to the outside for a smoke. I got talking to her, and told her that I was learning to be a healer and that apart from the circle I had not practiced healing outside of it. She asked me if she could be my first patient. I was nervous but decided to give it a go. I placed my right hand close to her eye my eyes were closed and I was carrying out spiritual instructions, my hand was there for about two minutes. I told her that there would be improvement the next day, spirit had indicated that this would be so. I told her that for the next two days I would give her absent healing, and that there would not be any more need for hands on healing.

Before I tell you what happened, I have to say that to all intents and purposes she would go about her life looking as normal as possible, dressed the same as any other person, with her guide dog on a normal lead. The next day she told me that for the first time in her life she was able to see the digits on her watch, I could have cried, I was so glad for her. Of course she was elated, I told her that absent healing would be given that night and that we would see further improvement. The next day she told me that she could now see down the length of the ward, through the window, across the lawn and through the hedge to the traffic on the other side, so now her sight was normal. I sought advice from the Spiritualists. I sought spiritual advice about what had happened. The reason being was that the surgeon who performed the operation was one of the best in this country, (he has since retired) and that we will always need doctors and hospitals. I was told that the operation was successful, and that the healing process normally took many months. So the healing I gave brought about the healing to that day. However my wife's eye problem could not be helped at that time.

Chapter 7: Two Good Men

Robert (bright Fame)

My wife and I first met Robert more than twenty years ago. he knocked on our door one evening and stayed for tea. We lived at that time in a council house in Bletchley. Robert was a very famous man not liked by many, but greatly respected by us. I found him to be a man of honour and integrity. he was a multi-millionaire, who came from a humble beginning, a family man. He fought the Germans in the last war, and was once honoured for saving a man's life. He was the sort of man you could approach if you had problems, he would always help you. The reason he knocked on our door was that he had heard through a person we knew that our son was in hospital and had been for some time and had at one point become seriously ill, caused through negligence. He took up our case with the hospital board and a few months later we were offered an out-of-court settlement. We refused the money, we settled for the fact that they admitted negligence, hoping that they would correct what was wrong. At that time we had little money but we were happy. This man showed spiritual feeling towards us and we were strangers to him. When Robert passed from this life, many people who did not know him said some awful things about him. His family have gone through hell. But my wife and I will never forget this giant of a ma, he will remain in our hearts forever. His name was Robert Maxwell.

His Lordship

Lord Longford is a man who is disliked by many people. Some people even think he is barmy for trying to help others like long term prisoners for example. This man has the sight to see within others, he carries on with his work regardless of the insults that are hurled upon him. For myself I think he deserves the utmost respect, for seeking the good amongst the bad. There is a future for this lord in spirit. Why do you think he carries on with his crusade? What do you think possesses this man? Within this man is a strong glowing light, spirit know him very well. He has a difficult task, and he is far from being barmy. I would like to meet him, one day I might.

Chapter 8: The Levels

Level One

On level one I've been told, all our immediate guides dwell. For me Little Bear. On level two my Shaman healing guide Silver Fox, on level three the philosopher Tey Lei, on level four Tejget the Athenian, other than these levels, there are five more, nine levels in all. Each level is better described as a level of thought. If on the earth you come to learn and understand thought levels, you could well pass over to a higher level, after first going through level one. My teacher of the levels, is a man from level nine. I do not know at this time his name or where he came from on the earth, or whether in fact he came from the earth. He told me that when the time's right, that I will be able to tell him who he is and where he came from. When I first saw him, he was dressed in a long off-white dress with sandals on his feet, I made a guess at who I thought he was and I was wrong. He has told me that when I return to spirit, I will either be on level two or three and as my learning progresses I will learn about all levels. Levels of spirit are best described as levels of thought, you don't go upstairs to each level.

On passing this life, we all return to level one, this includes all murderers and people with evil intent. On this level all re-education takes place. Here they have schools, for learning not only our past lives, but also learning for the future. Here you will be reunited with family and friends pet animals. After a short period of getting used to the fact that you are in spirit, your working life in spirit will begin. In spirit they have nurseries for babies, who on the earth were stillborn, miscarried or aborted. They touched the earth and returned home. In spirit they will grow to adulthood and they are named by spirit, with names they might have been called on the earth plane. They also have on this level animal keepers for wild animals, (they are not wild here), plus horses and farm animals, which are not returning to the earth. As more people on the earth become vegetarian the farm animals are becoming less in demand. When we are reborn our spirits enter pure, memories are there of previous lives, but can only be retrieved by regression. In spirit there is no such thing as evil, Satan, devil. The evil in a person on the earth is caused by genetic fault and how each spirit handles the situation determines what they have learnt in that life.

At this level there is much activity as you can imagine. All spirits here have to learn the mistakes made on the earth and probably more than 90% will stay at this level, before returning to the earth plane. When your spirits return they are as pure as a new born baby is and a task or a lesson will be learnt in each life, whether you return either as a woman or a man. You do not return as animals, man will not attain the spiritual level of animals for thousands of years. Spirits of animals are very special indeed.

When in spirit, if it's your destiny to stay put, then as your learning progresses it will be possible to attain a higher level. All spirits on higher levels of thought have got there on their own merit. I would not think that there is a man or woman born who would pass over to level nine. This level would only be attained by either someone progressing from level to level or someone from another planet.Spirits from other planets pass through level one on their way to a life on earth. As some of them get tired from living in perpetual thought and desire the material, they will only be able to do this until the earth reaches their planet's level. Equally when we pass over it will be possible to have a life on theirs. When I've learnt all there is to know about each level, then and only then I'll be able to communicate with the other planets.

The status of your life on earth will not go with you on passing, you will pass to level one the same as the rest. No private waiting rooms here for you, no servants either just love and kindness from humble spirits. No room on level one for your Rolls Royce, or lives of inequality. On level one you mix and talk with tramps and the people some of you turn your noses up at. But it won't be like falling from grace either. If your spirit has not learned anything from this life then your next life it probably will. You will be given the opportunity to choose your next life, you will know the outcome of this life, but will have no memory of it when you return. The lesson to learn in this life could either start at birth or just before you pass over, or if you are very lucky all your life. Imagine being royalty now and then passing to become a tramp in the next. Food for thought I think.

Level Two

This is one of the most important levels. On this level all prayers are answered, all healing requests are carried out on this level. Silver Fox my Shaman healing guide is here, and his band of loyal helpers. All the doctors and shamans await instructions from healers on the earth (physical life). We as healers tune in to our friends, who in turn transmit healing energies to us, mind to mind, and through our hands onto the patient. When we ask for absent healing the energies are directed straight to the patient no matter what the outcome is. Many hundreds if not thousands of problems can be solved here. I cannot put a figure on it, every day, every second healing is being given to someone. Every time that you hear of a miracle in a hospital and doctors have no answer for it, it's spirit that have stepped in.

Every miracle on this earth is brought about by spirit, it is not us healers that have the gift, we could do nothing without the knowledge of spirit. All of you that go to church and pray to God, it's level three that answers, they answer all your prayers and if they can help you they will. But they will not help you if you are just praying for a lottery number. They will not decide what side should win a war, in war they are on neither side. If you are one of the millions of people on this earth who just think about other people's problems, and your thoughts are given in a loving caring way, spirit will pick this up and act on it. Do not forget that spirit know every thought that you think, they never miss a trick.

On level two all healing guides dwell, they work in groups. The senior guide absorbs the healing energies from his group and passes them on to the receiver on the earth plane. If all parts are tuning in correctly then the power received will be enormous. There are thousands of senior healing guides and hundreds of thousands of assistants to them. If you are already a good thinking healer on the earth plane, then the chances are good that in spirit you could be a senior healing guide. It's not true that if you have had say one hundred previous lives that you would have learnt enough to stay in spirit. You may not have learnt anything. Progression to levels come about by a number of reasons. You can for instance change levels in spirit by your learning on level one. You will receive an assessment on level one, showing what your best points are. If the good far outweigh the bad then you will progress, either in a new earth life or by staying in spirit. There are no thoughts of leaders or masters here. Apart from the thought levels everyone is the same here. The words senior and assistants are only used to describe a situation, which can be more readily understood by us on the earth plane. The healers on level two come from all walks of life, and from all nationalities. Many of them however are Red Indians. Because for them while on the earth, they were more in balance with nature, they understood the spirituality of all living things. They only took out what was needed for food and clothes, by killing the weak and the old. In my words, I'll honour them by saying, that they are spiritually supreme.

Level Three

All minds of great wisdom dwell here. For my self, Tei Lei a level of philosophers. Giving advice and wisdom to all of those who can receive it. Every person on Earth will have a guide from this level.

Chapter 9: Out of the Body

Out of Body Experience

You don't have to be between lives to experience this, but you have to be spiritual. Firstly it takes a deep meditation, when I tried this the first time I asked for the experience and waited, to my amazement I found myself drifting up to the ceiling, looking down and seeing myself sitting in the chair and my bald head (partly bald). After returning to my body, I asked if I could experience leaving the house, this happened straight away, I floated through the wall and about 40 feet above the house, then drifted over the golf course which is adjacent to my house. I had no sense of weather conditions but I could see perfectly well. After a minute or so I quickly returned to my body and on entering asked if next time I could experience travelling. I felt very tired after the first two experiences. When I had the third experience I left the house the same as before and did what appeared to be around trip of some 20 miles in seconds or it seemed so. I remember floating over an airfield and seeing light planes on the ground, I also experienced speeding towards the ground and then swiftly up again, after returning to my body again I felt very tired and went to bed. I've had the experience and I will have it again when I return to spirit.

The Cathedral

During meditations I often ask to experience different things, on one occasion I asked if I could enter the spirit dimension and remember it. They duly obliged a few weeks later, they said I had to wait, because I was not ready. It was a strange feeling, I had to ask what was happening, they explained and I started my journey. The feelings I had with out-of-body experience were not the same this time, I had no sensation of changing dimensions this time. There was plenty of light, green grass, trees, gardens, blue skies. I was taken into a building with a man called Joseph, I could not see him at this time but had the sensation of his presence. I was not walking along but gliding along a corridor, against the wall were a row of nuns the whole length of the corridor with heads slightly bowed. I could see their faces but they were motionless their eyes appeared glazed, at the end of the corridor I was taken into a large area, which looked like a Cathedral. We were standing together looking forward as if from the altar, there were no chairs but about one hundred more nuns facing us, suddenly they all bowed right over and I was stunned to see that on their backs were white markings which formed a large cross. I felt who was I to see this wonderful sight, I was then ushered into a side room, that had a huge stained glass window. Then the person I was with revealed himself a man called Joseph, in off-white robes, a well established beard, curly hair not too old, mid fifties I thought. He was not directly looking at me, I cannot remember a word he said. I've been told since that this is normal. To remember being in spirit was a wonderful thing, I must not expect too much.

Chapter 10: Heaven Sent

One of God's Precious Souls

All day I have been hearing about this little girl who has cancer. This poor little soul has had more done to her than most of us have in a lifetime. The doctors have said that she is dying and has only a few weeks to live. That may be true, they have decided not to give her anymore treatment, because all treatment so far has failed and she has only been given a 10% chance of life. The main reason is of course money. In principle money should never come into deciding between life and death, the pain she will suffer must be considered. God alone is the deciding factor in life and death. It may be that her life is coming to an end, so she would return to spirit. In her next life she will be free of pain and her life will be full. Meanwhile I'm sending her healing and like her parents praying that she will survive, and live a normal life.

This is the Key That Will Unlock the Door

To recreate the fine balance of nature, we have to reduce world population by way of contraception. Re-establish forests worldwide, cut out all pollution. Find alternatives to nuclear power. Nuclear waste deposited now will cause havoc in the future. The alternatives are many, but less rewarding for the greedy fat-cats. The sun alone will give enough energy for the whole of this planet, only the instruments used to divert the energy cost, only one payment. Full central heating, lighting, cooking and hot water. This course of action alone will kick start the replenishment of our planet. We must recreate homes for the animal kingdom, which so many have lost through the greed of man.

Whenever you next visit a forest or the countryside think this, you have now invited yourselves into the animals homes, respect their homes, help to re-create the balance once again. Put back into nature what you take out, continue the cycle of replenishment before it's too late. If you feed one bird in your garden it would be a start. All zoos will have to close in the future, all animals returned to their natural environment, to rejuvenate this planet once again. Future generations worldwide will still have to pay a price for the stupidity of the greedy people. Your great grandchildren and all future offspring will pay the price of today's ignorance. Imagine all houses and factories where there were once fields, imagine no birds singing, rivers and seas so heavily polluted that nothing lives in them. In one degree or another this will happen, it's already started, stopping it is the problem. It must start now from birth with teaching from parents and when old enough from schools. In my lifetime alone there has been a tremendous change in attitudes, respect and discipline. We learnt when I was at school or at home

39

to show respect for your elders, they have the wisdom which will educate you. Discipline is a must, you must be punished when wrong is done. I enjoyed my childhood, attitudes so different from today. I can remember not worrying about locking your doors and being able to walk into other people's houses.

There was proper community spirit then, when people cared whether you were ill or well, alive or dead. But above all else we were a damn sight poorer as well, and this is the key that will unlock the door. If you have never had it you will never miss it. In 1953 my dad bought our first television, I wish he hadn't, because apart from it ruining family life, the radio was much more fun. In the east there are countries with high populations, but they are poor and still to this day have the key to our future, the only thing that they have to change is their population, which in turn will create less disease and reduce the mortality rate. The key = wealth = greed = selfishness. Answer = one class society, reduction in population, will this happen? Not until there has been world suffering on a scale not seen before. Suffering for centuries until the day dawns and the penny drops.

Just a Number

When people lose their identities, they just become a number. In this so-called modern world, a large percentage of us fall into this category. We become to be just like hole in the wall machines, waiting to be tapped of our limited wealth. Whether it be insurance companies, banks or any other financial institutions, they are there to suck us dry. I believe that sincerity from a person can easily be seen, in a simple handshake, often with bank managers for example you get a limp handshake, I'm always on my guard when this happens. With a bank account you appear just to be a number. True you get smiled at by an attractive bank teller now and then, but they don't give a damn for you as a person, whether you are alive or dead, ill or well. They are only interested in you for your money, paying excessive charges or high interest rates. Insurance companies offer interesting deals of one kind or another, but when you claim they will do anything in their power to avoid paying out. In their eyes we are all liars and cheats, and that we are making false claims, so it seems. I believe in honesty and fair play from all. I treat everybody with friendliness, this is the way it should be for everyone but sadly it's not. In time to come we will all be pure thinking, there will be no violence, wars, hatred, cheats and liars, only pure spirit minded people, hip hip Hooray.

Loggerheads

I've had a very bad day today, I've had people going back on their word, I've made appointments which have not been kept by the other party, money due has not been paid. All the worst traits in people I've seen today. For me it's very hard because as soon as I give a person a piece of my mind it creates a negative field and that's bad. For example, I had a man today deliberately try to force me into a traffic island, when I had the right of way on a roundabout, of course I gave way, but I was bloody furious, pointless though it is. It's very difficult being a Spiritualist and trying to run a business, and driving for a living. I'm at loggerheads with myself, trying to find the balance between my normal positive thinking against the negative feelings you get with other people. I'll beat it in the end even if it kills me.

Just Out of The Boundary

In Milton Keynes where I live, there are many country walks, lakes and wildlife where the various species of water birds can live in peace and harmony as nature intended. The only intrusion being the lens of a camera in one of the hides. Outside the designated area things are quite different. If any of these visiting water birds stray a little off course within a mile of the lakes, they get blown from the sky, by one of those nice country folk, with a twelve bore shotgun. They have no preference whether they be rare or not. Much more fun shooting clay pigeons. Among other things they call Milton Keynes the city of trees, if you ever visit Milton Keynes you will see why. Forget the concrete cows this is a place of great beauty. Along the side of a road near me there are Horse Chestnut trees planted in groups a few feet apart, imagine how glorious they will look when matured, there are millions of trees and shrubs planted everywhere some flowering and some not. It's a lovely warm sunny day today June 16th.

Along The Line

Have you ever noticed how stories being retold change so much from the original one. As they go down the line each person changes what the previous person said, adding their interpretation of events. If the line was only ten people long, imagine how the story line will change. The same can be said for writings, written long after the event. The Dead Sea Scrolls for instance, we are told that these writings started in 31AD. How much then of these writings are the actual truth. It seems to me that these writings could be exaggerated in a very large way.

Warrior Chief

How do people judge others to be savage? How do the Americans justify the slaughter and humiliation of the Red Indians, women, children, old and young, to say nothing about the slaughter of millions of buffalo. The great Sitting Bull was a man I would like to have met, a man of courage, humility and compassion to his fellow man. Long after the Indians lost their land. Sitting Bull went to work for Buffalo Bill, and a good percentage of the wages he earned was given to the starving children in the eastern cities of America. Sitting Bull now resides on level two of spirit, one of the many senior healers, he is also a philosopher.

True grit

The time has come for the liberated men and women of this earth to learn to forgive your enemies, for what they might have done to you. We must not keep reminding ourselves about the atrocities of war. We must learn to have peace in our hearts. To show true grit, forgive those you feel ill will towards. They are only people like you, they may have tortured you, but because of it, they too have lead tortured lives. They have had to come to terms with themselves and they like you need each other's forgiveness. Like you they had mothers who loved them too. Open up your hearts to one another and forgive.

Euthanasia

Spiritual destiny is the only thing that will decide your fate. Euthanasia is not the answer, all pain in this life can and is relieved either through medicine, herbal or spiritual healing. All life can be improved to give each of us a better quality of life. Spirit are the only ones who know the real reason a person or persons desire Euthanasia. What you think about is known by them in every detail. As already written about in this book, abortion is the same as Euthanasia, your desire to kill a living person. There is no life without spirit and as said before, spirit enters on conception. What are the real reasons that we dispose of life or desire it so freely. Normally for quite selfish reasons, immature love-making, causing unwanted pregnancy, where through ignorance contraceptives are not used. Because of some religions contraceptives are banned (but not enforceable). Through so called mistakes or having affairs. Unborn babies all have the right to live. Spirit are saddened by their plight and look forward to the time when this will be a thing of the past. Euthanasia and abortions are wrong.

Futile Battles

Man all through history has misused the meaning of the word God. When men fight wars, their priests ask for God's help, in inflicting pain and misery on their foes. Both sides in wars think God is on their Side. God is on everyone's side, but not in inflicting pain on one another, this is not the way of God. If man in wars gone by and wars now, had a piece of the higher knowledge, then there would never be a war again. Man could understand the true meaning of loving your neighbour. Politicians and some religions are the causes of wars, if all our armies shook hands with their foes and went home, the battle would be one for all.

Tei Lei

In a conversation earlier this evening with Tei Lei. I asked him about the time I was in the spiritual dimension and met the man called

42

Joseph (written about earlier in the book). recap I went into a building with Joseph, passing many nuns along a corridor. I was then taken into a very large room, where another group of nuns stood, they all bent over revealing a huge white cross on their backs. I was then taken into a side room, where Joseph spoke to me. At that time I could not remember what was said. I asked Tei Lei if he knew the answers to my questions, he said that he did. He told me, the significance of the white cross was, not as a cross of crucifixion as I first thought, but the ultimate meaning of the white cross was to show the total love and power of God. This was the reason I felt so humble seeing this sight in front of my eyes. Joseph was in fact telling me this in the side room, but on returning to my body I forgot.

Chapter 11: When Life Suddenly Changes

Friday the 13th

In time to come, I will be working as a healer and giving lectures on spiritual matters. I've been shown by my medium friend, over the past two years small glimpses of what's to come. I cannot possibly see how I'm going to get there, but my spiritual pathway is mapped out like everyone else. I was first told that I would be living north of Milton Keynes, and then a place where there are mountains. A few months later I was told, a white fronted house with blue window frames and then I was told Wales. The strange thing is that all my life I've wanted to live in Wales on a small holding, so who knows it might come true. In 1987 on Friday the 13th of February I was planning to go to North Wales, to view a small farm with the intention of buying it. The arrangements were made, and a hire car was ordered and was going to be delivered that evening. I was having dinner at about 6pm, when the milkman knocked at the door for his money. My wife answered the door and got into conversation with him for about twenty minutes. After saying goodbye to him, she closed the door and started to walk up the hall, where she suddenly collapsed, she was conscious and I lifted her onto a chair. She said to me that she thought she had had a stroke. I called the doctor who didn't want to come out, so I told him not to bother and that I would call an ambulance. As the ambulance arrived so did he, he said not to worry and that she would be home that evening. How wrong he was, my wife was carefully put into the ambulance and taken to the hospital. After several tests and admittance to a ward, at 11.45pm that night I was told that she had suffered a brain haemorrhage, and they could not operate for ten days, allowing time for the brain to settle.

After ten days she was transferred to Oxford Infirmary. When she could speak clearly to me, she told me that she didn't want to have the operation, mainly due to fear. I talked her into having it with the help of the doctors. The night before the operation as I was leaving the hospital at about midnight, I asked the porter if I could have the keys to the chapel, he duly obliged and I went in and prayed for her. This was the first time in my life that I had done this. I arrived home at 2am and a strange feeling came over me, it felt like all the weight had been taken off my shoulders, it was to be the first of many such feelings. My wife had the operation, it took about six hours. I arrived at the hospital as she was being taken to the ward. I sat by her and all of a sudden she had an epileptic fit, which is normal after such operations I called for the doctors and almost collapsed with shock. The doctors and nurses were marvellous and one week later she was transferred to Milton Keynes hospital, she was then sent home on Friday the 13th of March. With the doctors and spiritual healing she has survived some awful illnesses, I could write a book on her illnesses alone.

Chapter 12: Tragedy

Reflection

I write this part with a heavy heart. My nephew who is only 22 has just been killed in a freak accident under the wheels of a car. David was a young man any dad would be proud of. My brother Peter is of course devastated, my thoughts and love go out to him and his wife Kath. I wish I could give them a miracle cure for their pain, I will try. Grief is a lesson we all have to learn. David is in spirit now and in a few days I will be able to speak to him. He will be spending a lot of time now with his mum and dad, and all the family in turn, he will try to comfort them, my brother like myself will now be reflecting if we only did this or did that. David's life had reached its destiny, if it was not that day it would have been another, I'm afraid that's a fact of life. Men don't always admit their love for their families. I love David as I love all his family. Their pain is my pain, the woman driving the car, friends who were witnesses, their lives will always now be affected by it, and some will never get over it. One blessing was that he passed over instantly. Spirit have told me that they will give as much help to them as they can, by giving them healing thoughts. I dedicate reflection to my nephew and friend, David.

Five Days Later

My brother has said to me that he does not believe in spirit, he would if it could be proved. I had tried unsuccessfully to get a message from our eldest brother John, in an answer that Peter could accept. After five days in meditation David came to me with a very clear message, about what had happened. Until that point I had little knowledge of what had happened. He told me his friend had attacked him with a knife (his friend was mentally ill) as he tried to avoid the blow, he slipped off the kerb and into the road and the car ran over him. His words were these, he is my friend, he did not mean to do it, I feel no ill-will towards him. I felt that I would have to pick my time to tell my brother what had been said. The next night David came again and told me he was going to spend as much time as possible with his parents, with that he faded away. Two days later, I telephoned my brother to see how he was, he was now able to open his heart out to me. He told me about David's friends who had gone round to see him and Kath and at what they had told him. They told him word for word what David had told me. Once again, I was unsuccessful in proving the existence of spirit to my brother.

Chapter 13: Holidays

May 1st

I'm at Gatwick Airport going on my summer holiday. The very day of my nephew David's funeral. A very sad day especially for my brother Peter and his wife Kath. I'm sorry I can't be there, but as a Spiritualist I know that David will be, although not seen by most. Just before the taxi arrived this morning, I received a telephone call from one of my suppliers in great Yarmouth. The caller asked where I originated from and said that they thought I was from London, I said I came from East London, Walthamstow in fact, this was met with laughter from the background. A woman called Ellen was then put on the phone, and she asked whether I remembered a conversation I had with her a week before I said that I did. I had told her that I had given her husband absent healing the year before, when he was through illness, close to death. She then told me about a dream that her husband had, he said that in this dream he met a Pearly King and Queen (East Londoners know about these) they told him that a man from the East of London was going to save his life. The telephone call was confirmation of this.

May 2nd

The plane was an hour late and I've now arrived in Cyprus, this was going to be a day to remember. I was staying in Limassol and the front must be four or five miles long. I started my brave attempt to walk some of it, I headed for the old part of Limassol and on the way stopped and had some lunch. After this I walked close to the shoreline for a while and it was there that I was approached by a middle aged woman who said she was collecting money for a Cypriot spastic society. During the conversation she told me that her mouth was very sore due to some gum problem, I told her I would give her healing. She asked if I would speak with her later when she had finished work.

I was to meet her at a coffee bar outside the place where she said she lived. I paid her some money and agreed to meet her, I already knew using my own intuition that something was amiss here. I was enjoying a cup of coffee when she arrived with her son, she sat down and asked the waiter for a menu, she ordered a meal for her son and one for herself plus a strawberry milkshake, I thought who was going to pay for this. The food arrived and after one or two mouthfuls she called the waiter back and complained about the food, in all the waiter brought her three main courses and two milkshakes and she still complained, she could not be reasoned with, with the waiter or me, she was then told that unless she left the cafe the police would be called, she promptly left taking a handful of food with her, of course she did not pay I offered to pay the cafe the money but they refused to take it, they said it's on the house.

They said that this woman always bothered tourists pretending to be working for the spastics, and using the money for herself and that she was a prostitute. I still gave her healing, I was not going to judge her it was through circumstances that she was the way she was, I would have given her the money even if she had not lied. For me this is being spiritual.

May 3rd

I'm off on a cruise today to Israel and Egypt, I'm not sure in what order.

May 4th

Israel

On a rushed guided tour of the religious sites, I thought I might encounter some spiritual feelings, but this was not to be. I was only just able to say a short prayer in the church where the manger is. The only heart-warming thing I saw was a huge gathering of children, all girls, pretty as a picture in their uniforms and paper hats going in two's through the manger. The sights seemed so unreal, no likeness to how it would have been, even the church had no feel to it. There were security guards flitting from place to place arguing with some of the tour guides, with raised voices.

We were told that May 4th was the day of Independence in Israel and there were many celebrations going on. Most cars were decked in their national flags. The worst aspects of a guided tour, was the behaviour of the adults, rushing and shoving their way to the front of the queue, for the best position for themselves without a thought for others, the orderly way of the children should have been noted by all. The tour guide quickly rushed us to our coach, to take us to a shop in Bethlehem, to spend our hard-earned money on over-priced goods, and with this goes the constant demands of the roadside sellers, trying to sell you the pictures of the very things you have been taking pictures of. More time was spent at the shop than there was at the manger, sad isn't it.

At least I was able to pass the place of burial of our friend Robert Maxwell on the Mount of Olives.

May 5th

We are given a police escort across the desert at high speed, from Port Said to Cairo. Parts of the desert have been cultivated using irrigated water from several canals in the area. Cereals and citrus fruits are grown in abundance here. The Egyptians are very happy and are a very polite people. The farmers live in humble houses, they dress smartly in their gowns and turbans, the Egyptians probably call them something else. We were first taken to the pyramids at Giza, but were not given enough time to go into the

47

Pyramids, as the guide wanted to rush us round the monuments, so that she could take us to the shop. So all in all the experiences I expected were not to be. The spiritual experiences are what you see around you, and not in things of the past.

May 6th

Back in Cyprus, whole of this day spent relaxing. I've been unsteady on my feet since I was in Israel caused by pressure in the ear, like you get when flying (in planes that is) I've given myself healing and I'm sure it will pass. While staying at the hotel I've met three English people, and one of these people was suffering from an acute arthritic problem, I gave him healing and told him so, I also gave him the address of Harry's house so that the healing could continue. If the quality of life improves for him then it would have been worth giving him healing, as for my own feeling of being unwell, I'll live to fight another day.

May 7th

Slept late and missed breakfast. Walked along the front until it poured with rain. I found a nice English pub and had Sunday lunch - roast beef, runner beans, carrots, Yorkshire pudding (lovely). After lunch I went to the zoo. Several types of animals live here, although the zoo would get ten out of ten for cleanliness, the sizes of the cages left a lot to be desired. In one small enclosure there was an Indian Elephant, with room to turn around just. The very next enclosure contained an ostrich, but the enclosure was three times the size strange I thought. One cage had four lions in it, the cage was in two halves four males one side and four females the other. Another cage had one tiger and one lioness in it, very unusual. Next to this were two Siberian bears, bored out of their minds, nothing to do except pace up and down and stare at them strange people trying to feed them with peanuts in their shells. Would any animal lock another animal into cages, to live a life of utter misery forever. The answer is of course no, their spiritual intellect far exceeds us mere humans. When a man can attain the spiritual levels of animals, he will then and only then have reached his peak.

May 8th

Going home today, VE-Day, back to reality.

Chapter 14: Heaven Sent

AC/DC

At this moment on the earth, there are more negative thinkers than positive. The reason for this is, that most people take life for granted, they think that they have God's given right to all things. They are the people who sit on their behinds waiting to receive things from others. They are the complainers too, the ones who find every fault imaginable, who always look on the down side of life. Negatives are the takers as well, give nothing only take. If the word and its meaning could be removed from our minds, we could all become positive. Positive thinkers have the world at their feet and are on the first rungs of the spiritual ladder. Being positive brings strong vibrations and friendliness from all.

Free Spirit

We are all free spirit, we choose what we desire and try to plan for the unsighted future. Although we possess this free spirit, for many women on the earth the 'free' is repressive. All the way through history some women are looked upon as slaves to men. Not I hasten to say in the liberated eighties and nineties in the west. But women in the east and far east are looked upon quite differently. Because in many cases of religion women cannot show their faces in public, not the will of God but the will of man. God created women to show their external beauty to all. With free spirit they would be able to do this. Also in parts of India and China women are considered to be the lower forms of life. Thousands of women in these countries are forced or obliged to abort female babies, just because they are female. Ignorance and selfishness go hand in hand with repressive spirits. Women the world over need to be more liberated, they need to have a say in their own welfare, they need to be equal in body as they are in spirit with man. Women are not the dregs beneath our feet 'they are free spirit'.

A Little Light

There is a little light in all of us, regardless how we live our lives. In this respect God made us equal, and this light represents the good that can be found in all of us. The mentally insane, the child molester and child killer, they all have a little light. The light shows itself in all of us. by the way we do things in life, which normally would not be apparent to anyone else. Because it comes from within your spiritual self. A child killer may have a deep down resentment of a child, possibly reflecting something in their own lives, where they feel that they have to inflict pain on others. Because they have suffered in their lives, not an excuse but a strong possibility. Although this sort of person can inflict injuries and death on a child, at the same time they can show complete love for an animal, or for one of

49

their parents. They can also perform some very compassionate deeds during their lives this is their piece of light. Most religions cannot see or find this light in all. William Booth had a huge amount of this light and in his day, as to this day that light has spread all over the world in kindly deeds. He could see, he had the vision to see that light in all men, in every person upon this earth. His work continues in spirit and on earth. For myself this is what religion should be about, the true love of your neighbour and all living things.

A Buddhist priest is another example of this light, they have inner peace, they only think positive thoughts for all. Have you noticed their happiness, the Dalai Lama for instance, he never stops smiling, not just good manners, he has that inner sparkle, that comes with understanding the light and what it represents. When you can understand the truth of this light, when you can feel its warmth, then and only then you can say that you are one with God. When that day comes you will start to experience the inner peace that goes hand in hand with this knowledge. Most Christians will say upon reading this, that they already have seen the light. But what they see is only a small part of this light. To attain the whole light you have to have the spiritual knowledge you have to see the good that comes from the bad. You have to see that little light within every person on this planet. Your thoughts must always reflect the love you have for your fellow man. When you have achieved this level, then you will be able to say to yourself that you are at one with God. As said before this takes us many lives to understand and each life is a progression on the last.

Please do not misunderstand what I have written here, especially about religion, you must if it is your will to pray and sing to God. God will always be around you, whether you understand the power of the light or not. This is only a guide to the higher knowledge, much of which has been bestowed upon myself. The knowledge I possess has given me the insight of the eternal light which we all possess to some degree, in earth life and in spirit. It never diminishes, it flickers on forever.

Love

Love is the best well known meaning of spirituality. Love means spirit, love controls the emotions of all man and all living creatures. When man can understand the meaning of the word love and what it represents, then the ultimate would be achieved. Love can be described in many ways, for example mentally retarded children, born with genetic fault. Sometimes being born from women who have had their children late in life. You could not ask for more loving children, who grow up as children all their lives. They are very close to spirit all their lives, they are also close to people, it makes me want to hug them. They are very close to the power source of spirit. As they remain as children all their lives, they remain close to God.

Animal Magic

Animals do more for us than you think. Dolphins for instance are kept in small numbers in marinas and spirit would like to see more released. Dolphins can and do work wonders for people, especially children. There is a place in America on the coast, who use Dolphins in their work with children, with children who have difficulty in speech. If the child does well with their teachers, as a reward they swim with dolphins, who become the immediate tonic they need, the dolphins know this, they are very good communicators. The pity is that when some of the children are taken away from this environment, they often revert back to the way they were. Spiritual healing may be the answer for them.

Minds Full of Debris

All people on this earth suffer with their minds being filled with debris. If you could learn to clear your mind of all the negative input, you would fast learn the advantages of positive input. The types of debris we carry around with us can best be described like this. Am I going to wake up on time, will I get to work on time, my neighbour is not going to repair the fence, my neighbour has allowed his garden weeds to overgrow into my garden. The neighbours are having a party again and are making too much noise. Will I ever have enough money to pay all the bills. Will I ever win the Lottery or the pools. My husband or wife is staying out late again, are they having an affair. All these thoughts are what people think about from time to time. What we have to do is place them in a positive order, for example, will you wake up in time yes if you have set the alarm properly, yes if you have gone to bed at a reasonable time, yes if you have not been over-indulging yourself with drink the night before. Am I going to get to work in time, yes if you have not done any of the above, yes if you leave early enough to allow for the unforeseen.

Perhaps your neighbour has fallen on hard times and cannot afford to replace the garden fence, or that he is unwell and has neglected his garden. The party may be for a celebration, a birthday, a wedding or an anniversary. You may one day win the pools or the lottery. Your husband or wife may have met an old friend on the way home, and got talking, or perhaps had a drink. it could be that their car broke down on the way home in the middle of nowhere. Positive answers to what might have been the reason. We need to communicate with each other more often. Ask your neighbour are you well, could we share the cost in replacing the fence. I heard that you are celebrating a birthday, so I have bought you a card and I hope you enjoy yourselves, you would more than likely be invited. If you won the lottery or the pools, you might even have a street party to celebrate your good fortune. Make sure your car is properly serviced and that you belong to the AA or the RAC or something similar. Be sure to telephone home if you have been delayed for some reason, common sense really. If you do not do any of the above then perhaps you have something to hide. If you can achieve positive thinking, then think how much better your life will be.

Defeating the Object

In many hospitals in this country, the standards have dropped alarmingly. For example, patients are sent home too early, to do their convalescence at home. To be like it or not a burden on their families, who have to carry on with their lives the same as before. Go out to work come home and care for the sick person. When the responsibility is with the hospitals. Not that you do not care about the sick, but the strain it puts on yourself is not right. When did the hygiene rules change, one minute the nurses wore hats and no earrings, with their hair done up high on their heads, and then it all changed. No hats and wearing jewellery with hair hanging all over the place, has it been washed I wonder. Doctors seem to if they wish not to wear white coats, using their own clothes instead, does not say much for hygiene does it. You can on occasions see blood on floors in the casualty departments and bandages with blood stains on them on the floor, with other patients in and out the same cubicles. In times of HIV and low standards there has to be a question mark concerning the recovery rate.

I find it quite strange that hospital staff and visitors to the sick are allowed to enter wards, feeling and being ill themselves, coughing and sneezing over the very people who are trying to get well. These same standards also apply to doctor's waiting rooms. You first of all have to make an appointment to be ill on a certain day, and then have a long wait because the appointment is not kept. When you arrive at the surgery you are told where to sit, and then you find yourself sitting amongst equally sick people passing their germs to everyone. A better system is required here, where more qualified people nurses not doctors, can do home visits to people with contagious diseases. Only trouble is it costs money, and it seems that no-one in government want to spend any more on people's needs. They prefer to spend it on self-indulgence with their entertaining for the boys. When they clink their glasses at each other with their smug grins, do they think about the appaling legacy they have caused in our hospitals, 'no' of course they don't, they might say cheers henry are you going to join us on the hunt old boy, representing well our government's one class society.

A total change of thinking is require here, the ministerial old boys brigade has got to change. The very people who are on the bottom of the scale are the very ones who put these jumped up wasters in power. The majority are the have-nots, so the have's are the ones who must change, before our one class society can have a chance. The wasteful money redirected from government waste to the national health service. Bring back the standards of long ago, put care back into the community and mean it. The have's are normally out of touch with reality, because for them they have private treatment, no waiting lists. The old boys network is still very strong they know how to close ranks when it suits. Our leaders are the ones who only have to spout words, not join the queue at the job centre. Not be on the waiting lists for years, not knowing where your next meal comes from. These people who are supposed to represent us, what a right shower they are. Some of them most certainly think that they are Christians, they do not know the meaning of the word. Would they share a part of their wealth with a tramp, what would they say if they were entertaining and a tramp knocked on their door (if he could get through the security system) he would be told to bugger off or something similar, they would turn their noses up and offer nothing.

To have a change of thinking has to start from the top downwards, from the ones who have most to lose materially. To put things right in society you need action not words. There must be someone in government with the sight to see the problems and good ideas on solving them. God willing they will come to the fore soon and start by putting their own house in order. They could firstly wake up the sleepy house of lords and stop the waffling in the commons. Then to make the cuts in it's own spending to the bone, not to award themselves any more pay rises for at least five years, to set an example to the rest. There should be no free handouts to those who work in government, I write work loosely. Your holidays should be no different to anyone else, none of you should skive off your responsibilities to the electorate.

These words are said to you as spiritual advice, look within yourselves at who you really are, are you someone to be respected and trusted. Do you always tell the truth, do you feel anything for others. Be sure of this, spirit know you better than you know yourselves, every thought that passes through your mind is known by spirit, your self-worth will only be known by spirit, I wonder how many of you will have learnt anything, I would guess very few if any. No one party is being singled out, this concerns everyone in government. When you are next at a cocktail party, suggest to your host that perhaps it would be better if we had a cheese sandwich and a glass of inexpensive Bulgarian wine. This could be your first saving, wine £2.95 shared by two, cheese sandwich £1.00 or a cheese doorstep £1.50. Much has been said in this chapter, straight to the point is the best way to be. I feel sorry for those of you who risk their jobs by opposing the leaders of your party. So much for a democratic country.

Genesis

We are taught in our schools and in books that man evolved from the ape man. This is not correct, we originated from Mirranda. To evolve to what we are today. We evolved from a race of people, who are so like us, there are only slight differences between us and them today. Ape type creatures did indeed exist, but only as the forebears of the apes and monkeys of today. These creatures like us were placed here. The apes at that time walked upright and they had an intelligence level similar to ours. The species were all different sizes, their spiritual level now being much higher than ours. The pecking order then was gorilla, orangutan, chimpanzee, baboon, gibbon. Their forebears faces were similar to that of a gorilla of today, they were more bodily hairy. When we first came from Mirranda we were exactly the same as Mirrandians in every detail. Our brain capacity was much larger then, a more supreme being. But as each 1000yrs past we gradually changed and with that change started to decline, on the spiritual and intelligence level. From 5000yrs - 2000yrs BC we had become what we are now. From 2000yrs BC - 1900yrs AD we slid into decline.

The signs of a revival are with us in this century. The trouble is we have been in decline for 4000yrs, and only in the last 95yrs have we started on our way back. The animals though have not at any time been in decline. Their thought levels being higher than ours, has allowed them to remain the same. They have no need of material possessions like us lesser souls. Look how the mighty gorilla can show so much love and compassion not only to their own kind, but also to man.

A Couple of Bob

Why do strapping young men beat the living daylights out of old men and old women, to rob their purses of a couple of bob. Have you ever wondered what makes these people tick? It makes you wonder whether they have mums or dads and grandparents. Are they drug crazed thugs or do they get pleasure from inflicting so much misery. This type of crime is caused by the breaking down of family discipline. In some of these families there seems to be a couldn't care less attitude. Where the parent or parents constantly swear in front of their children and behave very badly. The consequences being, that the child learns from their parents, so if for example the father beats up the mother, they think this is normal behaviour. It seems to be becoming a way of life with youngsters today. To put this right is not an easy task. It might be a good idea to send parents back to school, they may learn something. Another alternative is, when one of their children are involved in criminal damage they should be made to foot the bill, regardless of how long it takes to pay it, even if they have to sell all their possessions, they would soon straighten them out then.

54

If the parents were sued every time one of their children attacked someone else, discipline in their family would soon be used. It's no good people saying that he or she comes from a broken home so what, that's no excuse for mugging some poor old dear. Instead of patting their hands and telling them not to be naughty boys, and giving them probation or community service they should be placed in a corrective military establishment, where a bit of square bashing will help them enormously. Drill discipline into them, what with their parents footing the bills and them square bashing they would return to the fold normal people.

Do Gooders

There's nothing wrong in doing good for others, but the line has to be drawn when prisoners are thought of more than their victims. The victims families suffer all their lives and they are constantly reminded by the media of the perpetrators of their pain. The criminal of course can feel remorse, but will never feel the pain of the families left behind. Do-gooders in this sense, do more harm than good. The criminal has no rights when violence on another is committed, they forfeit all rights to normality, when this action is taken. The sentence for first degree murder should really be a life for a life, in these enlightened times the law prefers life imprisonment. Life imprisonment should mean life, with no rights whatsoever, no visitors, no wages, never to breath fresh air again. You now think that spirit are hard and not caring, you are quite wrong, the spirit within is learning a lesson in this life. The fault of being a murderer is genetic, not spiritual. The life the murderer chose when in spirit was in this case to be a murderer and to perhaps feel the anguish she or he has caused. Their spiritual thoughts will be assessed after passing. Do-gooders please do good for the right people for the right reasons.

The Making of a Better World
1. To give of yourself (not money)
2. To help others in thought and in deed
3. To turn the other cheek when offended
4. Not to inflict cruelty on animals, or any living thing
5. To accept spirit into your life
6. To keep in daily contact with them
7. Think before you make profits from your spiritual gifts

Not the commandments, but seven good thoughts, one for each day of the week.

Spiritual Facts

God exists as the creator of all life, on this planet and all others.

God is neither man nor woman.

God is pure energy (white light).

Earth people originated from Mirranda.

Man did not evolve from apes.

We have all had past lives.

We all choose our next lives.

UFO's are real.

Mirrandians, Athenians, Opugnians, Orrellions, are real people not war-like, or violent.

Ghosts do not exist (only spirit forms).

There is no such thing as the devil or Satan.

There is only the feeling of love from spirit.

Life is everlasting on earth and in spirit.

We are all born telepathic.

All animals are telepathic.

It is possible for all people to communicate with spirit and in time all other planets.

It is possible for all people to communicate with animals.

Life in spirit is a life free of all pain.

Family or friends will meet you on passing this life, and take you across.

Chapter 16: Heaven Sent

Evacuees

During the Second World War, thousands of England's children were sent off from their homes, to the safe haven of the countryside. Their parents bidding tearful farewells to their life's blood, not knowing where they were going or who with. Apart from their relief of sending their children away from danger, this actual act took great courage. The children settled in with strangers, who offered their homes and families to them and showed them much love and protection. These acts of courage and love were brought about by war. But it shows the true spirituality of people where needs must. We are all capable of being like this.

Brain Dead

How many times have you heard people say? they behaved like animals. These thoughts or sayings are very negative, animals are far more better behaved than us mere humans. To put thugs on the same level as animals is an insult to them. Animals do not ever behave like us, their genetic and spiritual make-up is far more superior than ours, best to choose your words more carefully. Why not say that he or she acted like a brain dead person, this brings it more to the point I think.

Blame

Who do you blame, for the loss of work that so many poor souls suffer from in this country, urban decay comes about for a number of reasons, it might be as a direct result of government action, or for allowing British manufacturing companies to close, in favour of cheaper third world imports. Many whole families have over the years trained to become a skilled work-force, only to find themselves placed on the scrap heap like their over-worked machines, with little prospect of finding new jobs. Smaller companies have opened up in the place of the larger ones only to be closed down again as the recession started. It normally results in total despair for normal working folk not being able to keep themselves. Once proud men start to despair of their lives and family it starts to breed resentment of the better off, who are normally out of touch with reality, where do we begin to search for the answer.

The government of this country have left it far too long. Someone needs to encourage English companies to expand into run down areas, companies that can offer training and take on large numbers of people, regardless of age. However many companies prefer to expand in third world countries for cheap labour. They should be prevented from doing this until we have got our own house in order. They must be made to realise the consequences of their greedy actions. When people are allowed to work again, their self respect will return.

Born Again

During many lives on earth, people reach a point in their lives when suddenly their lives and thinking change. This comes about by spirit entering our minds to bring about the change. People who do not understand the world of spirit often call themselves born again Christians. Although they reach out to the church and probably remain in spiritual ignorance all their lives, a change takes place in their thinking. Where they start to see the world and its people in a different light. It makes them feel happy and content and that must be good. For some though they misunderstand what has happened to them, some poor souls see a spiritual light and think its aliens, although this might be true in certain circumstances. The difference between spiritual and alien light is plain to see and feel. For the rest of us spirit lead us into new lives, by making it possible to meet certain people who lead us on our spiritual pathway.

Some of us have been given the sight with our eyes closed and open. On the other hand most people have their eyes open all their lives, but see nothing. Born again sight is not seeing every day sights, it's seeing and feeling all around you, every living thing, it's knowing and not believing. Born again Christians are believers and knowing should apply to all Spiritualists, but sadly it doesn't. Some have been given the sight, but are still blind, open to prejudice and cruelty in their lives. They have yet to find the spiritual balance in their lives and will spend most of their lives seeking it. It's all too easy to slide back into old ways, for all people to be born again, is learning how to see.

See Sense

Spirit need you to understand some of the previous chapters, the ones that will seem to be hard hitting. You must not take any of this writing as a personal insult, or a judgment of any kind. Much of the contents of this book apply to life in general, I myself am no different to anyone else. I've had as many negative thoughts as anyone else, I'm no angel. But at least I've learnt to understand and profit from my spiritual knowledge. Anyone reading this book has the same opportunity as myself to gain the higher knowledge and by doing so, to change your thinking for the better of all.

Getting the Hots

All the way through this year from February to now the end of October 1995, my wife has been seriously ill. She has been on the brink of life and death. She has been admitted into hospital four times, she has a heart defect. While she has been under the hospital, spirit and myself have been giving her healing which has helped her both physically and mentally. Although she has received the healing this year and other years we have not been able to cure her. But we have been able to improve her quality of life a little. While the healing of my wife is not brilliant, this year I gave healing to a child with leukemia and she has made a total recovery. When the hospital said they could do no more. I'm very concerned about my wife this night, as she has suffered bad chest pains, when doing little things, like moving a chair. So this evening spirit and myself have given her enormous healing, which had the result of totally draining myself of energy which left me very tired. We wait and see the outcome of the healing.

During healing of this kind, the heat transference is very hot indeed. When healing was asked for I was told to fix my eyes onto the ceiling above the lounge, where my wife was sleeping and to imagine staring straight at her with my eyes closed. They told me that I was going to get very hot and that this feeling was to continue for five minutes. Well they were true to their word, I felt like I was cooking. As soon as the healing stopped I started to cool, in all healings that I give there is always a change from cool to medium hot feeling. If a person placed a thermometer on me while the healing took place, it would not move one degree so I'm told, yet I sweat buckets isn't it strange. I also get this feeling in church when spirit come close to me.

One day when I went to a Sunday service I was sitting in a hall among about twenty people, the medium was giving messages to other people, when suddenly spirit came around me, I started to get hot, they said to me you're next and I was. Speaking for myself I've no need of messages from church mediums anymore. All my messages come direct as said before. I'm able to communicate with everyone that I know in spirit and all my guides that I did not know. Many Spiritualists go to church each week look forward to their messages. For newcomers it's fascinating, if you go and find it interesting then delve a little more deeply and join a circle you may be pleasantly surprised at the outcome. Discovering new found talents that you never knew you had, like healing and clairvoyance, even a healer is a medium.

Ancestors

The link through our families bloodline, is purely genetic. Each person's spirit is completely different. You may trace your families history back several centuries, but the only link with them is genetic in this lifetime. In your next life you will be somebody completely different with a new bloodline. The memories that are stored in your spiritual mind, can be tapped in any life you have. The history of your spirit can be revealed at will, by being taken back (regressed). When you do this, it reveals many of the lives that you have lived, whether you have had a life as aristocrat or beggar. In the few lives that I was taken back to, I have been a peasant farmer in the times of Henry Tudor, a royalist fighting and being killed in the Civil War, a very wealthy aristocrat and a manager of a printing company. In all those lives lessons for my spirit were learnt and I've advanced to how I am today.

Sacrilege

I once said to someone when you look at a tree what do you see, the answer back was as much as could be expected. The person said, I see a tree it has leaves and branches, it's wood. I said that when I see a tree I see a thing of great beauty, regardless of the size. Through each of the seasons the tree stands out proud, in the summer with its many shades of greens, in the autumn as it sheds its brown leaves, what a glorious sight, a nuisance to some, but giving that picture postcard look. The same can be said about winter when there is frost or snow on the branches the trees always look magnificent, then comes spring with new formed buds waiting to blossom out. So does it make you wonder when so much damage is done to our trees, through thoughtless urban development. Where countless thousands of trees that may have stood in splendour for 100 years or more are treated so badly, felled because they are in the way for that bypass or building. I look at it this way, the mature trees were there first, bypasses and buildings should be built around them, not through them. Woodland should remain woodland for all time. if all the trees in the world were removed, we would all perish. Each tree is as important as each person, it's up to us to protect them from danger, and to make sure that none are felled for the sake of money. I love trees, it's a wonderful feeling when walking amongst trees in a forest or wood, there is so much peace there, cutting out traffic noise and where you can find yourself more in tune with nature. In woodlands you can do much thinking, without being disturbed. So if you are ever asked this question you will know the answer.

If you already think this way then you have the beginnings of insight. These same questions can be applied to animals. For example, if you asked someone to look at a cow in a field and then asked them what do they see, most would say that they see a pint of milk or Sunday lunch on the table. What they should see is a beautiful animal, gentle, loving, caring, watch the suckler cows in a field with their calves, see all the best attributes of nature. When man is able to look at other life and see within, then the turning point would have arrived. I would like to see more schools teaching children from an early age to respect all life. To be educated and encouraged in the planting of saplings. To explain to them that young trees sometimes between the ages of 3-7 years are being damaged by children breaking off branches or worse still bending them over till they break, educating them from infants will help them all their lives. They need to be taught the

60

consequences of their actions especially to the amount of wildlife that depend on young saplings and then trees for their survival. When children are young they can take in this kind of knowledge. At this age they care about more things than when they are older without learning. I beg you to think more about animals and trees and all wildlife, to understand and care about what's written in this chapter, will make you a better person and you will be admired by spirit.

Without Consequences

Most people live their lives for themselves and their families, without thought for more important matters. For example, most of us go out to work, we work hard for our earnings, husbands and wives working all day and meeting for a few hours in the evening. Weekends are sometimes spent away, if it can be afforded or spent in the garden or DIY. This routine is carried out every day of the week. Topics of conversation mainly being about one of the many soaps on television or perhaps about someone else, who can't answer you back. Then it's off to bed and the cycle starts again. If you were able to stand back from yourselves and watch the way you carry on, you would wonder to yourselves what life was all about. We work and play all our lives actually not accomplishing much at all. You may have bought a house or a brand new car or you might live in a cardboard box. Stand back and look at yourselves, understand what you are doing and ask yourself why.

To understand what life is about you have to have a change of thinking, to understand the spirituality of man. When you can understand spirit you will begin to realise what life is about.

Humility

Self worth is measured many ways by ourselves. Some people assume that self worth means how much money they have, their status in life, how many feet have they licked on their way to the top. Maybe because they own a Porsche or a Rolls Royce, most people judge self worth to be material possessions. Well for all of you that think this way, self worth means good thinking and good deeds to your fellow man or any living creature and a respect for all life. As in the previous chapter, to prove your self worth a change in thinking is required.

Chapter 17: The Planet Suite

UFO

Since the days of the ape cave dwellers, there has been sightings and landings of people of other worlds. There have been numerous sightings throughout history, century after century. As we approach the 21st century, sightings and landings are becoming more common place. Why do you think that is? According to some UFO societies, there will be a mass landings by the end of 1997. This remains to be seen. While talking to some people from another world, I thought at first that I was talking to a group of Mirrandians, but as I was to find out I was quite wrong.

Mirranda

Mirranda is the planet where people of this planet came from, a huge planet many times larger than Earth. Like Earth a planet of great beauty, where there are no wars and nature works as it should. In my search for more knowledge I asked spirit for the chance to communicate with someone from Mirranda. It worked like this, the spiritual dimension of Mirranda, is different from ours. So a medium in our spiritual dimension was used to transfer information to me, through to my mind. When I asked for this experience, I expected it to take many months, mainly because I thought I was not ready, but to my amazement it happened one evening not long after asking. Two people were talking to me, one man and one woman. I received a vision of the two people, something like, looking at a negative photograph. The two people were in floor length gowns, which appeared to be black or dark coloured, and with buttons down the front, top to bottom. Their heads were bald and a slightly different shape to ours, but all other features the same. During conversation with them they told me that they were in fact from another planet, and that they had made Mirranda their new home. They also said that they were more technically advanced than the Mirrandians and that their people were used for all communication.

I was told that the Mirrandians were the same as us. At this time I'm not sure about Mirrandian's races or colour, or what planet the communicators come from, but I will do before this book's finished. I was told that the average lifespan in earth time was between 150/250 years. They get over the population problem by a more advanced form of contraception. They only produce offspring when the balance of population changes. Most couples only have one child, for them it's a way of life and it works. They also have rivers, seas, and forests like us but on a larger scale. The animals that live there are never culled or mistreated, they have much respect for them. The animals lives are shorter there, than they are on earth, for this reason the balance is kept.

These people are in our terms light years ahead of us in learning. They have learnt to live in harmony with themselves and all living things, and conflict is beyond their thinking. They have also told me that their planet has two suns. So next time you see a UFO in the sky it might be them. Not being warlike, like us, they will never hurt you, they are merely here to observe us. I will add to this when I have more knowledge.

Opugnion of the Solairnum Galaxy

Mirranda and Opugnion are both in the same galaxy, that they call Solairnum. The communicators I spoke to about Mirranda as I said came from another planet which I have now learned is called Opugnion. They told me that their planet is much larger than Mirranda, and that their planet shares one of Mirrandas suns. They also have another larger sun, to warm up such a huge land mass.

Both planets also have two moons, I've found it increasingly difficult to communicate with these people, as I always fall into a deep sleep, but I shall keep trying. They have so much knowledge to give, that I don't want to miss any. Here we go again, one of the communicators has told me his name, which is Eelo (pronounced ee-loo) a man. He has told me that his planet is under-populated, and that many of the planets inhabitants live on other planets. A part of their planet, as big as Earth is all desert. The rest of the planet is similar to Earth and Mirranda. It has huge seas and forests, and an abundance of wildlife. The animals are never killed for fun or food the animals live their normal lives on their planet. They eat some vegetation Eelo told me, the Opugnion's that is, their normal food is beyond our thinking but he said that they produce their own food by using a form of energy, the energy come from within themselves. The food has all the nutrients they need, but by way of change they eat vegetation hot or cold, if hot they generate heat themselves, something like the healing energies that I receive through my hands. They do not marry like us, but the love of a woman is bonded in the same way. Unlike the Mirrandian's they can have as many children as they wish, their planet will never be over populated.

Eelo gave me a colour vision of himself this time. In earth years he looked to be in his late twenties, clean shaven, bald head and blue eyes.

Eeloo

Update, all communication between earth and all other life forms will come about through telepathic means. Teachers on the earth will in the future have special schools, so that they can learn how to do this. My spirit friends have taught me how to do this and it is possible for all of you to learn in this way. But as many of you will never become spiritual, schools will be available for you. Scientific minds will learn also, they often talk on the television about space travel, fuel and the cost of it, they often speak of distance from the earth to their planets, in light years. We must put thoughts of Star Trek and time as we know it to one side. With the help of our alien friends they will show us how it's done. With their advanced technology the travelling to and from earth is much quicker than you think, the cost zero. When the earth is ready for this advanced technology it will be given. before that time comes all thoughts of violence and conflict must be banished from our minds and a change in thinking will only bring this about. Earlier in this book I mentioned my thinking on travel through thought, to recap I was told that this was partly right which it is, but I also understand that there is a breakdown of energy, solid matter. These two things coupled together bring about this form of travel, first you see it, now you don't.

Travelling from one dimension to the next. We have to stop thinking about time as we know it, because it only exists on earth, we on earth only talk of light years away and can only imagine travel using the fuel we use now. Eeloo and his friends can communicate with us now using telepathy, in any language, the same as our spiritual dimension. They look forward to our enlightenment, when we have learnt spirituality the rest comes easy.

Going Forward

The spiritual progression of man has steadily increased through the 20th century. If we went back in time to say the witches of Salem, the witches were mediums, they were able to communicate the same as we do now. But because of ignorance and superstition, they were burnt at the stake. In the years 1900/1940, mediums in this country, to attract people had to create fantastic feats. For example, being bound with a rope to a chair and then have spirit remove the jacket from under the rope and then the whole thing being reversed. (Jack Webber). Or huge tables being lifted off the ground and then moved at high speed across the room. 'Till now in the nineties when to demonstrate the power of spirit in such a way is not so important. If we were to go back in time to say between the years 10,000/20,000yrs BC, the Athenians and at 20,000yrs BC the Orrillions, these people from other planets were then, is how we will be in years to come. It would be true to say that when man reached the pharaoh era, man was starting to decline. Through the 20th century we are just starting our long climb back. As each decade has passed in the latter part of this century, more and more people are becoming aware.

Towards the end of the next century 2090 awareness would have grown tenfold the world over. As environmental issues grow they will create more awareness within. By the middle of the next century, great spiritual strides will have been made. With up to 40% increase in understanding. Every decade of the 21st century will become a great event spiritually.

Gradually we will become more higher thinking, leaving the material behind, we will start to become like the Mirrandians, Athenians, Opugnions, and Orrillions, it will be a wonderful time.

Xanthus

Sounds like a Greek name does it not, perhaps there is a connection somewhere but I doubt it. When I was given the opportunity to talk with these people from another planet, they came across to me to be very similar to us, the exception being that they were much smaller than us. Their features were very much like ours, nose eyes and mouth, but no sign of ears, their average height being about 4 feet. They had picked up my thoughts on thinking that they were Mirrandians, and between them had quite a giggle about it. They confirmed what I already knew about earth people coming from Mirranda. They said that Mirrandians are the same as us in every detail. They told me that they came from the planet Xanthus being the nearest pronunciation in English of this name. They told me that their planet was 159 yrs from earth, that's light years in our time.

The Xanthians are a very sensitive people, very loving in an earth sort of way, they have an intelligence that we cannot even dream about, they came across to me as compassionate caring people. All communication is telepathic, and they were to tell me this about their planet and them. They said their air on their planet was extremely thin compared with ours, and for that reason their internal organs are completely different to ours. They cannot possibly survive in our atmosphere as we could not survive in theirs. They said that their planet's terrain is similar to some of the earth's, and that they do have a limited amount of running water, but I feel that they have no need of it. They spoke to me about space travel and how amused they get from watching us. They explained how they travel like this, that in space as with earth each existence is a dimension of thought and that travel is possible at beyond our comprehension speeds, through inter-dimensional travel, so by travelling through dimensions your objective is reached in no time at all. In some UFO clubs I've heard it said that they think that other planets have bases under the north sea, what nonsense, if they can travel here in minutes why have bases/ Before our meeting of minds finished they said that they have landed on earth many times and that they have left the ones that had passed over behind. I wonder if that had anything to do with Roswell.

Chapter 18: The Levels

Level Four

The planet Orrillion has two moons and one sun, and this planet is smaller than both Opugnion and Mirranda. These people are responsible for the daily welfare of their own kind and their spirituality. They are there to communicate with their spirits who have chosen to live on earth in earth bodies. The thoughts are relayed to them in the same way as ours do to us. Sometimes it's a wish by their peoples to live a life on earth, in a material life. So their guides or masters dwell on level four, to give them guidance and spiritual welfare. Athenians on this level do much the same, except that they help with the communication between earth people and other planets, by acting as mediums for other planets' spiritual dimensions. So that when a link is made for myself to speak to Eeloo, the Athenians tune into Eeloo, who in turn passes on spiritual messages, mainly normal chatter and also through his mind he is able to produce images from the Athenians, which in turn are passed onto me. They are there to assist us in our higher spiritual knowledge, for us to learn about their planets and their universe.

John

I had a brief talk with John about level four and he told me there was little more to say about it. I told him that I could not imagine what sort of information was going to come about from levels five-eight. He said that this was perfectly natural, and that from time to time they would give me ideas to work on, much of the information would come this way, and when I was ready I would know, and communication could resume. I said to John that I thought that animals must have a communication level, the same as us and that the answers were on one of these levels. His answer was that I was thinking along the right line and that I will understand more when the time was right.

Level Nine

Level nine is for pure thinking spirits who have learnt through their own endeavours to think only the purest of thoughts. Gone from their minds all traces of negative thinking. This level of thought can only come about by ascending the levels in spirit, you cannot obtain at the moment on earth this state of mind. They are able to see all problems associated with us on the earth plane. They are able to act as teachers to us and to other guides on lower levels. They are advisors to earth people an the people of all other planets. Any problems with other planets are resolved through negotiation from level nine to the planet concerned spiritual dimension equivalent. Only special people attain level nine. Just realise this, 100% of world population return on passing to level one, almost as many return to earth for new lives, a minute percentage remain on level one and an even smaller percentage rise to level two or three.

The highest level you could expect to attain with we will say 30 years of spiritual learning is level two or three. What sort of person are you that rises to level nine? I think it's safe to assume that all the people mentioned in the Bible, including Christ, would not have gained any more spiritual status than you or I. Christ would have had some negative thoughts during his life, if he had only one negative thought that would have prevented him from reaching level nine. On level nine the white light resides, on this level is the power to control and teach all levels, all guides and helpers, on this level is the power source. For the millions of creatures that do not return to the earth because of loss of habitat or extinction all go as spirits into the white light, and in there they enhance its beauty. All spirits are treated with love and respect here man or animal.

Level Five

On this level your spiritual future is decided, assessments of your previous spiritual lives are made here. From here your next life will be chosen by you, your lessons of this life and the choice of families that you will choose from is decided from level five, it will be the same lesson no matter who you choose, if you are to remain in spirit your assessment will be made here.

The Levels Update

My teachers have informed me, that the knowledge passed onto me concerning the levels, that these are brief accounts of what happens there, and that all this knowledge is out of time. So rather than tell me things that I need not know, I'm only told some relevant details of each level. The rest of the knowledge can only be obtained in spirit, should you be lucky enough to rise to any level above one.

Chapter 19: Heaven Sent

Chance Meeting

Often meetings are arranged by spirit for people to meet. For example I was out canvassing for my business recently and on the route that I travel there is a hotel and restaurant, which I had thought about canvassing at some time, so one week I stopped there and parked my van at the front, but I suddenly changed my mind and drove off home, to this day I don't know why I did this. The following week I decided that I would stop there on my way home. After trying a fruitless canvas, I had a drink at the bar and got into a conversation with the barmaid. It started off by talking about things in general and about out interests, I said to her that I was writing a book and of course she asked me what it was about and I told her. She kept on talking about spirit and didn't want the conversation to end, but knowing the subject like I do you can talk about it all day and night.

During our talk, her friend from round the corner came in and went into the bar opposite, the barmaid told me that her friends son had been killed recently, in a car crash and that her friend would be interested in talking to me. A few minutes later her friend approached me and asked whether I could help her. So we sat down and she asked me several spiritual questions and during the conversation, she said that she had no intention of going into the hotel that day, but as she was passing she suddenly got the urge to go in. I'm now helping this lady to come to terms with her loss and her grief. So you can see that there are stronger forces at work here. All my spiritual work comes about in a similar way, I do not have to go looking for it, and I do not have to wait for people to come to me. Spirit normally arranges meetings for me. 'Who needs a secretary'.

Mirror Images

When babies are born, we all have dreams to what we think they are going to grow up like, we all think they are going to be someone special, and that they are going to have a better life than we had. The reality is normally quite different. If they are not given the discipline that you perhaps had in your young life, then what hope of a decent future for them. They are mirror images of yourselves, if you bring them up correctly in a loving environment. My son for example was brought up to show respect for others without my wife or I ever having to hurt him in any way, even as an adult he will often ask our advice or give us some, both ways mutual respect. He has grown into a normal caring person, I can remember when he was at school and he was nearing a time when he could leave school, some of his friends were leaving school and bragging to him of what they would be able to buy with their wages. My son wanted this for himself, he asked us what we thought, we said to him that if you stay on at school for another one or two years and passed your exams, you would be able to get a more worthwhile job, and that your friends might become a part of your work force. Needless to say he stayed, and then won an apprenticeship and is now a manager of a small company. With the right teaching your children can be more than mirror images, they can be yourselves.

Truth Will Always Out

Spirit have always been true to their word about all the writings of this book. I have learnt in the past few years not to scoff at anything that they talk about. If the scientists of the world today could start to learn about their own spirituality, to understand and accept it, then just think about all the untapped knowledge that is available to them, answers to many of the problems before them, perhaps they have spent all their working lives on and have not found the answers to them. Spirit possesses all this knowledge, and much more besides.

Most will scoff at this statement, but I tell you now, they are wrong. For the ones who do not doubt this statement, you must look within yourselves to find your self worth and what it amounts to. Get some spiritual guidance from a spiritual church and learn how to communicate. You may be able to do this within one year or you may already without your knowledge already possess some ability now. Just imagine a spiritual answer to that nagging questions. The answers to all problems is there for the asking, the only time that it will not be given is when the answer is out of time.

The Motive

Some of the writings in other chapters of this book is concerned with the greed of man, and to what lengths he or she will go to achieve this. In England for example laws were changed to make it possible for public houses and large supermarkets to trade all day, every day. Breaking up normal family life, but of course this does not apply to the large supermarket owners, who have their feet up as usual on Sundays. Now they are trying to have British Summer Time altered, hoping to make more money from leisure activities and not considering how it affects other people's lives. No doubt the next thing on the list will be for businesses to be able to trade around the clock. When all the avenues have been exploited what happens next. Companies are allowed to become too large, they take over at will, smaller companies often providing better quality and then shut them down, so that they can corner the market and perhaps make even more money, while the work force join the ever-growing dole queue, with not much outlook for future employment.

Families come under pressure from mortgage companies, for the money they have not got, rows start, families break up, all for the sake of money and the greed of it. While the bosses congratulate one another on their good fortune. The larger supermarkets of this country have been allowed to destroy the smaller independents and their suppliers, Butchers, Fishmongers, small grocers, bakers, newsagents, deli's, off licences, petrol stations, to name but a few. When will it all stop? It will stop when the ordinary folk of this country realise that all the shops that they could always rely on are gone. Cast your minds back to when you could walk into a small shop and be spoken to politely or when some of you were short of a few bob and were able to receive credit with no interest. Where the shop keeper would know you as a person, and would care if you were unwell.

Now compare this with a supermarket, you will be lucky if you get a smile from the checkouts, and if you want credit you will have to produce your piece of plastic, and you will not be asked if you are alright, you won't even be remembered, when you next go to that store. What is happening now is the beginning of breakdown in our society. It causes people to show no respect, or caring for others. Only the changing of thought, will change this course of self destruction.

A Person's Wealth Is Assessed By Not Considering Money

Much has already been written on this subject, but it becomes the bone of contention continuously. The lives of most of the people on this planet revolves around financial wealth. A rich man becomes even richer when he without being prompted gives a little money, to a less well off person, because the deed, has greater value than the money. If all of us can give to the needy without being prompted, by for example the television, we will all become that much richer and the good deeds that you do are often returned by spirit themselves. If a very wealthy person gave nothing to anyone else in the way of deeds, then the pauper who does is far more wealthier. The poor man who gives will never be forgotten by spirit, they will always look out for you, by monitoring your life and stepping in where they can. Deeds can be described in many ways, it very rarely involves money. You could for instance, all of you help someone by caring about them, even if they are strangers. A smile works wonders for all people, even that small gesture is a deed.

Spare time to talk to lonely or elderly people, don't let them talk to the four walls of their rooms, if you only speak to them 10 minutes a week, a deed that will be highly regarded by spirit, you might even find the conversation interesting. If you know a lonely person, offer to take them out for a drink, or invite them to your house, maybe for dinner or lunch, your rewards will come in this life, and in spirit. You can extend these good deeds to all forms of wildlife, trees and plants, you could try what prince

Charles does and talk to them, (I'm serious). The greatest earthly thing that anyone can give is time, but most people are always chasing the clock, rushing to and from work, husbands and wives working different shifts, children and pets to be fed, washing and ironing and all general housework to be done. Slow down, why overtake the car in front only to be caught behind the next, for miles on end. Be more leisurely in your life, and find time to do those good deeds.

A Heavy Heart

A short while ago as most of you will be aware of in the UK, was a terrible disaster, when the Sea Empress went aground. With the amount of incompetence surrounding it and the huge loss of wildlife, it makes you wonder what sort of people allow these catastrophes to happen. All the people in charge just shuffle their feet and do little to prevent damage to the environment. What for I ask? You can bet your bottom dollar that money is the key. When this first happened, I tuned into spirit and asked if they would intervene and help protect the wildlife, the answer back was, that people had to learn from their mistakes regardless of the amount of damage and death to wildlife, I must say that this answer hurt me very much, perhaps I expected too much from spirit, they said that its a part of my lessons, too. It's not that spirit do not care, far from it. Because their thinking and understanding is on such a high level, they see life on the earth plane as just an interlude. Virtually all the wildlife that have perished from this disaster will return from spirit to a new life, almost as soon as they leave this one. So the cycle continues.

Hopefully soon, someone will take responsibility and offer a solution, where money is the last thing that's thought of. Whoever is found to be the blame, must cough up the cost of putting it right, even if they go bust because of it. I find it quite strange that these disasters waiting to happen are always close to wildlife habitats. Goodness knows what's going to happen to the fishing industry in the area. At the same time as complaining, we give praise to the men who are working hard in their endless battle in clearing the spill from our beaches, and those wonderful people who give so much of their time and effort cleaning the oil from bird's bodies. I think that the ships owners should be with them doing their bit to help the wildlife. When this is all over I hope to God that it's never forgotten and that people have learnt their lessons well.

Who Tells the truth?

The above applies to every person on this planet. Most of us at one time or another would for some reason only known to themselves have at least said a white lie. Have you noticed for example when people in the public eye are challenged by the media they always deny any accusations

71

that are put to them, denial and counter denial and when the truth is finally out blatant lies are exposed. Why do people do this? What are they trying to hide? They would receive far more respect if they told the truth in the first place. Blatant lies going on unchecked will lead to other problems, lies are very negative, lies breed contempt from others, lies = corruption, dishonesty, leaving you with no self-respect. People who lie about the things they make believe they own or occupations that do not exist, just to impress someone, a girlfriend maybe or someone you have been introduced to, who already possesses what you are lying about. Fancy job titles are given today for people who collect our rubbish and who clean toilets, for whose purpose is this for? Be proud of what you are and what you have achieved, no matter what job you do stand up and say it out loud, as long as you can be honest about it to others and yourselves. For you so-called famous people, for once in your lives tell the truth, when asked those awkward questions, you will be a far better person telling what you might be ashamed about and you can walk away with your head held high keeping your own respectability, even if you think no-ones going to know, spirit will whatever you decide.

It would make a nice change that when people who are in the limelight are interviewed on the TV, to answer directly and not to evade the question. Because this again becomes an untruth, that's why in this country leaders are never taken seriously by the electorate, they lie about their manifesto's and they avoid truthful answers to questions. They tell you how they are going to make other countries envious of our status in world standing and then put as many people as possible out of work. They then deny responsibility for their actions and blame others. One thing's for sure, they won't win any brownie points for truthfulness. The most common lie with us normal folk is, that we tend to build an illusion around ourselves, trying to make out what we are not, these are the general run of the mill white lies. Some might say human nature, but the real human nature is to be the opposite of this.

We need to be more honest with ourselves and change this image we have built around ourselves. When you are all reading the contents of this chapter, the thoughts you have on the subject and your reaction to them, will be known, and how you evaluate them and draw your conclusion will also be known. This chapter is giving everyone of you the chance to readdress yourselves.

When The Penny Drops

When eventually the penny drops, all of mankind will think quite differently all thought will be of a pure nature. All mankind will be totally equal, a total one class society, where the understanding of class to us now will not ever be thought of then. With this change of thinking will come the end of all conflict no more rich and no more poor. The starving people of this world now will have their stomachs full, their dignity and an overwhelming feeling of love. This way of life will become the norm in the future. Where religion in the true sense of the word will be no longer thought of, but a new spiritual way will be understood by all. We will become like people of other worlds, with new technology beyond our present thinking. We will be able to, all of us to communicate through telepathy with all other worlds and all other dimensions.

This planet in the future looks very rosy indeed, just imagine a world where we will never have to worry about the environment again, where every creature on this planet will be able to co-exist with us for all of their natural lives, where we will never have a desire to kill another creature again, whether it be for food or sport. Where we will never have to worry about that planned bypass destroying wildlife and our beautiful trees and plant life, where the motor car does not take precedence over all things beautiful.

From The Heart

If I was like I was before becoming spiritual, and on knowing what was going on in Bosnia, I would be calling the Serbs to put it politely total riffraff. These people being the perpetrators of so much suffering, the killing of the innocents, women and children mainly Muslims. As the truth of what happened starts to emerge we have to wonder to ourselves, whether these people are human. Well they are, but with only a flicker of their spiritual light within, as they do not seem to have any compassion for their fellow man. They lack the basics of spirituality as do so many people today. These types of people are the ones who take great pleasure in inflicting pain on people and animals. One type of person who falls into this category is the badger baiter, wickedness to the extreme. These people are without the basic qualities that make us what we are, they like the Serbs seem to have something missing from within. But on their return to spirit they all become overwhelmed with kindness and love, that they themselves could not offer when on the earth plane. Where one might think that a punishment is more fitting, its always the opposite in spirit, even with spirits of the very ones that they might have killed while on the earth they will receive love, kindness and forgiveness from them. Many of you will not be able to accept this and I quite understand this, with a change in thinking now, or your next trip to spirit, you will understand.

Now Tell Me This

Why do people from all walks of life wipe their own excrement on toilet walls. Or why do the majority of people fail to wash their hands when they have used the toilet, even is they are preparing food for themselves or others. Or why when out in the countryside do they discard litter, paper plastic bags, beer cans, or soft drink cartons. Or when they are visiting their local public house put out their cigarettes on the carpet. Or when they go to the toilet again they never pull the chain, but manage to put a lot of it on the floor. Have you ever noticed the amount of litter by the side of our railway tracks, and some that has been thrown over the backs of houses and onto the embankment. These being the worst traits in human behaviour, does it make you wonder what it is like inside their houses. This brings me on to the moan a lot brigade who complain about the owners of dogs. who allow their animals to pass what comes naturally onto the grass. It seems to spirit that it is us humans that have got to get our own house in order first.

Why not use the labour of young offenders to pick up the rubbish along the side of our railways, it would be like the fourth bridge never ending, every railway track that I've been along is covered in rubbish, there is probably enough rubbish to fill a couple of thousand trucks, I bet. Please understand this, countryside, forests, lakes, rivers and even man-made parks are all places for wildlife and animals in general. It is perfectly natural for animals to pass fluids and other matters into the ground. The wildlife habitats are their home, not ours. We impose on them, as we impose ourselves with so called free spirit on everything, with total disregard to nature and the balance of it.

Chapter 20: Christians

Jesus

Some Spiritualists call him the Nazarene, I call him Jesus. Jesus was born from the seed of Joseph and the womb of Mary, just like you and I. For the best part of his life, he lived it, just like us waiting for that moment when his work would start. The last few years is what he lived for, the helping and teaching of others, to give of himself, free without profit. To heal the sick in such a way they were called miracles, much like today. I'm writing this part on his birthday, the one day I celebrate the same as others. I'm a Christian Spiritualist, I know Jesus lived, He was a healer, I'm a healer, God is the creator of all.God is neither man nor woman, God is pure spirit, pure energy. God is God for all people every living creature, tree or plant on this planet and all other planets. Jesus died on the cross, through the ignorance of others. A lesson he had to learn, a wonderful caring person who gave everything, what a waste. If people then had the wisdom of spirit, how much better it would have been for him.

Our God of Light

God is neither man nor woman, in spiritual eyes, God is a beautiful white light, pure energy. The creator of all planets and all life. God created love for humanity and created a fine balance in nature. Every living creature depending on another (except man the destroyer of all). There is no heaven or hell, as we are taught as youngsters, heaven and hell is what you make of this life on earth. When looking for God or praying, don't look up to the sky, there's only sun, moon and clouds there, and rain is you live in England. God is around us all the time in the beautiful flowers and trees in everything you see that's living. When you pray for help, it's the spirit people who come around you, trying to give you support and help where they can. The white light is a wonderful thing to see, in meditation I've only seen it once, I felt honoured.

Non-Alcoholic Spirit

In churches and temples, all over the world, men and women gather to pray to God, to worship with singing and prayer. Mostly kind souls, religion is always difficult to talk about, because someone always gets offended. Wishing not to offend anyone in any way and not standing in judgment of others, who feel their way is right, I will make these comments. We all pray to the same God some talk of Holy Spirit or Allah. If only all of you could understand spirit as a whole rather than a holy, there would be no need to go to church. God's church is outside, where the doors are always unlocked. No need for expensive buildings in cost and keep, or for a large vicarage, for small families. Or the pomp that goes with fine clothes or gowns, depending on their rank. Where church leaders waffle on about the poor or some other topical issues, from their luxury apartments or the pulpit. It's no good talking about good things in church, where you believe God is, and then be the opposite when leaving.

The wealth of some religions leaves a lot to be desired, when you think of the amount of money wasted on status alone, instead of using it to help people. They are some of the bad points, but there are many good also for instance, the Salvation Army, what wonderful spiritual people they are, bringing help to the needy all the world over, highly regarded by spirit. Also some of the vicars who open their doors to their houses for the unfortunate people who have nowhere to live. Nothing is ever missed by God or spirit in general. If just one person reading this book, who is living a grand life helps someone else for the first time, then it has been worth writing it. Apart from the Salvation Army, I've deliberately avoided naming churches and religions. The reason being that you know who you are. Think deeply about what's written here. When praying ask (friend please help me to understand) and you will.

Exorcism

The church have their own way of exorcism, I once read somewhere that they sometimes think of spirit as demons or trapped here, and they are freeing them and sending them to God. In fact they are neither of these. When we all pass our bodily life we will all have the opportunity to inter-dimensional travel, going back to places and people we loved on the earth, and sometimes haunting a house or two. You will be able to move things around, some people or spirits are able to speak with a voice but normally it would be through someone else on the earth, so all communication would be through telepathy if they have learnt how to do it. As for exorcism I have tried it on a couple of occasions with some success. Success only in the eyes of people who do do not understand, for example, I could ask a spirit to be more quiet and this will result in the people concerned thinking that the offending party has gone. But they all have the right to be wherever they want to be and providing there is no harm done what's wrong with that.

I was once watching a programme on the television about a man who was haunting a pub in the north of England, and not being of the same thought as I am now, I tried an exorcism. The man who was doing the haunting was a man who had murdered a child within the pub and buried the body in the cellar area. Because of his troubled spiritual mind he was unable to leave completely. So I asked for communication with him and encouraged him to leave and return to what was left of his family in spirit. It was to become a memorable experience. After entering into a deep medita-

76

tion, I asked him to return home to spirit, where love and kindness were waiting for him, where in fact forgiveness had already been given. I asked him to go back through me and into the light, I will never forget the feelings that went through me when this took place. His pent up emotions and the overwhelming thoughts of love and forgiveness that was coming from spirit to meet him halfway was very emotional for me, I actually felt the surge of his spirit coming through me. I was quite frightened at first, with goose-pimples all over me, but I soon felt what he was feeling and I felt elated for him.

Chapter 21: Latin

Patria, Our Native Land

Some of the injustices of this world are slowly being resolved, i.e. South Africa, Middle East. The main countries that suffer now, are the ones that are run by tin-pot dictators. I feel very deeply about the impoverished Africans, of many countries in the African continent. I often send them my healing thoughts, I wish I could do more, my heart is saddened by their plight. Often the West looks on, but does nothing until the next famine. South Africa is one of the richest countries in the world, some of the wealth needs to be diverted, to build reservoirs in the poorer parts of Africa, free of charge, it would be nice if some generous people did this. It would be giving back some of what's been taken. We have to replace, replenish the land. These people are entitled by God's law to live with dignity, with love and peace of mind, with their stomachs full and their children free of disease. These things are the norm in the West. Spirit would like to see a more constructive effort for these people and more education for contraceptives. Will all the readers of this book send loving healing thoughts to these people. I'm positive they will receive them, and that the thoughts will help them. The same applies to the animals of Africa, where man continues to interfere with nature. By the greed of nations wanting ivory.

Fortunately the world ban on ivory is helping the Elephant population for now. The hunting of the Rhino for their horns, is a disgrace. I feel the Chinese have much to learn (I know my guide is not offended). They are the cause of so much suffering. The remedies they seek, they could get from spirit or by the use of more roots and leaves by using them for infusion. This is much better than misery for animals. The answers to all medical problems can be found, without causing suffering to the animal kingdom.

In the Presence of (Coram)

Whenever I tune into my spirit friends, I feel that the above title is very apt. When you can master the technique of tuning you will feel very humble in their presence. It does not matter what status they had on earth be it prophet or pauper, their presence is felt. Although it is natural for us on earth to feel this way, in spirit you do not feel this way. The differences between spirits is in thought only. When guides speak to me through a trance-medium they always say it's a great pleasure to meet with you again. When I do it for myself, my guides call me by my first name and as I communicate regularly first names suffice. John as I call him, my teacher of the levels, makes me feel in the presence of, as does Joseph. I once felt this while learning in a circle. I was given the honour of seeing the prophet

Elijah, rather than seeing coloured lights and animals. At first his back was to me and he was pointing to another man in the circle, and saying to me, tell this man he has the ability to be a great healer, tell him that the power from my hands are for him. I asked him who he was, and he swung round, a huge man, with huge hands, a large head with curly grey hair. He had a large forehead with deep-set eyes (brown), he boomed at me I'm the prophet Elijah and with that he was gone, and I've never seen him since. The man he was referring to was in fact a very good healer, although he did not think so.

This is what he did for me, after my accident, the next day in fact. I went to the circle as usual, with a heavily bandaged right arm. My arm was black and blue and quite painful, after the meeting had finished, he led others in a joint healing for my arm, he laid his hands on my arm and for some strange reason my ears started to pop. The very next morning the pain had gone and when I took the bandages off the black and blue bruises had gone, so he had the power.

A Thing Desired (Desideratum)

Material and spiritual fall into this category. It's not wrong to want material things, spirit understand our earthly needs, to them material is unimportant and spiritual welfare takes precedence over all. But we have to live our lives ruled by money, getting your spiritual lives into perspective in a material world is very difficult, it can be done, but only by a desired change of attitude of yourself. For a complete change of thinking. Believe you me, it's not boring at all, I'm occupied daily with spiritual work one way or another, when time allows tuning into spirit takes much time. In the blinking of an eye, so it seems, an hour has gone. I find tuning to higher levels, brings about tiredness which you are not able to control. Many times falling into a deep sleep, after talking to my guides and then after waking up, not remembering a word said. However this is a normal reaction, as your entire self is relaxed. Try it if you dare.

Omnia Vincit Amor (Love Conquers All)

God created love for all mankind, and all living creatures, for mankind to be able to love everything. All of us on earth love someone or something, whether you are a murderer or a saint, the most fabulous gift man can have. Love helps us to strive for the things we want out of life, whether they be living or material things. When the love of material things is wanted i.e. a new car just like the neighbour's, or a house. Envy, love, jealousy are all the words which motivate people. But love motivates more than anything else, you show love, by buying things for a loved one jewellery, clothes, or tickets for a show. The love of a man or a woman is expressed by making love, making love gives pleasure, and makes people happier, so love in a relationship creates many things. The love of a pet creates a bond between you and them. A dog for instance will respond to a person who loves him or her, even to a person who is cruel.

A dog will always do its best for you, by jumping into freezing rivers, to bring back the stick that's been thrown in, not for the dogs benefit, but for yours, they always greet you when they have been left for hours on their own, or left to cook in the backs of cars, never complaining. If people could give as much love as a dog can, just think of what could be achieved. it's from animals that mankind can learn about love. All creatures give of themselves, without greed, selfishness, and hate, their whole lives operate around one word and that's love. Man on the other hand desires too much and most are guilty of this if not all. Do not put the love of the material before the love of the living.

Afresh Anew (De Integro)

If any of you who read this book and feel enlightened with it's contents. Start along the road yourself, you will most certainly feel fresh and a new person. Your whole outlook on life will change for the better, and as you carry out the work for spirit, you will be aware of their closeness to you. If for any reason during your spiritual life, you require help and guidance, they will give it to you. You will find that if you work for them, then they will work for you. It's a nice feeling knowing when they are around you, if you become a healer the rewards are wonderful, when you can see the change in a person who has suffered greatly, then there's your reward. I sincerely hope that some of the readers of this book, start out on their spiritual pathway with a higher knowledge and do some good with what they have learnt.

Chapter 22: The Levels

Level Eight

On this level dwell the overseers of all plant life on our planet and on others. They are responsible for the regeneration of all species, by monitoring the climate, wilful destruction and to suggest in the minds of those of us that can do something about it, in ways of putting the balance right. All plant life as we know it are self seeding, even species that have been long extinct are in seed form under the soil, ready to spring back into life should the climate or whatever placed them in this situation, changes. Although all plant life including all trees have spirit within them, it's not spirit of the human kind. They remain on the earth's surface for all time. For an example of regeneration in Egypt desert soil with no apparent plant life will all change when irrigation takes place, plants not seen for generations suddenly appear. It's not only spiritual learning that level 8 dwellers obtain, it's knowing the earth's and other planet's ecosystems that give them the right to dwell here.

Who Is This Man

I have only two more thought levels to write about. The man I call John told me that I will know who he is, when I've finished writing about the levels. At this precise moment I have not got a clue to who he is.

Level Seven

On level 7 the animal power source can be found, from this level all aspects of animal spiritual needs are taken care of on this level. The power source is not of human origin. As the spirituality of animals is far ahead of ours it is very difficult for me to understand. From what I understand all animals are born with this telepathic ability, especially among their own kind, I do not know whether there is any communication between them and spirit while they live on the earth. We will as a general rule in the future be able to communicate with animals telepathically. At this time I have no other information on this level.

Level Six

This is the final level I will write about. On this level a collection of the best minds dwell. The spirit who dwell here have only level nine above them. The thought level six covers all aspects of spiritual thought, these spirits are the advisors to all other levels, for the guides and their helpers, advice and decision making when necessary is made here. Level one can receive guidance from levels two, three and four, levels two, three, four, five and eight receive guidance from level six. level six, seven and nine run their own levels, they do not answer to any others, other than God. Who these great minds are I do not know, maybe I never will. As I began to receive information on this level, I knew from thoughts given to me earlier what my teachers name is. Up to this point I had no knowledge whatsoever to his identity. It is a great honour for me to have this truly spiritual man as my teacher. Since I have been learning about spiritual matters he is the only one that has been already written about in the Bible. he is the prophet Elijah and you can read about him in the book of Kings. Much of the knowledge I will learn will come from this man. As mentioned before I first met this man while learning in a circle, he came to me with a message for another person, I felt at the time that there was a greater reason for him being there and now I know why. Why me I cannot answer, no doubt he will tell me when the time is right.

A few weeks later he gave me an answer, he said this, (when I told him that I felt honoured at his presence) you have no need to honour me, I am the same as you, I'm not the great man that you think I am, I feel and think like you, I'm humble.

Chapter 23: Miracles

Man or Miracles

Sai Baba is the man of miracles, I hope so much to meet him one day. He lives in India, in the Bangalore region, he was born of his father's seed the same as Jesus. Like Jesus he was born to be a great man in his adulthood he is able to perform the most miraculous healings, blindness, cancer to name but a few. He is able to place one part of his body in one dimension and the other in this dimension. Why this man is not well known I'm not sure, possibly because most of his work is in India. Should any reader wishing to know more about him, you can buy a book called (as above) Sai Baba Man of Miracles. This book is a very interesting read.

Miracle Workers

The Catholic Church can so I'm told create saints if a person can achieve two miracles. Miracles happen every day, many as the direct result of spiritual healing and all miracles happen because spirit make them. In his time Harry Edwards was a famous healer, he like other healers brought about through the help of spirit healings or miracles every day of the week. How come that he wasn't made a saint?

Every healer on earth can and do make miracles happen every day, all healers however know that power comes from spirit alone and that they are only the receivers of the energy. When spirit are seen on the earth by people who do not understand, often shrines are built around the sightings, many sightings are seen as biblical people. You must understand that the sightings are of normal everyday souls, who for one reason or another are drawn to that particular area. When people pray at the shrine, they pray for, that hoped for miracle, it is often given. it comes about by the thought energies that are sent out while praying. Spirit are drawn to these energies and if they can help you they will. Another point worth saying is, that most people only pray to God when all else has failed, this is not wrong, but it might be better if asked for first. The difference between people who pray for help and a person who tunes into spirit is this, when people pray they are not aware to whom they are praying. They do not understand the spiritual dimension and that power is transferred by thought. The person who tunes in does, he knows that the power comes direct from his or hers healing guide, that thought transference is the direct result of all healing.

The miracle makers all live in the spiritual dimension and in the minds of some on earth who are on ego trips. Many healers will remain in ignorance of the power source, the gift being given to them for reasons only known to spirit. In some countries and in some churches healing is given by priests or preachers by placing their hands on the persons forehead and then they push them over onto the floor. This course of action seems very strange to me, silly nonsense from people who do not understand the power source. I ask you why would spirit want to risk pushing someone onto the floor it might cause serious injury. This is for effect only, people become hysterical when they witness this rubbish. The power source is warm. comforting, compassionate, caring, loving, they are your friends for all your time on earth. Some healers get recognition on television for their healing and get inundated with requests for help, which of course in fine. But let me tell you this, that on this earth there are thousands of healers who get no recognition at all, all their lives and they perform with the help of spirit, miracles every day of the week. The true miracle makers.

Chapter 24: Heaven Sent

The Void

I know in my heart that the time is fast approaching when I will have to step into the void, and quite honestly I'm afraid. Although I'm becoming more spiritual by the day and that I know that my friends in spirit are always near me, the fear of that step never leaves me. I imagined this scenario before I became spiritual. I built up a small business from nothing and I've been doing it for the past 13 years. But through the recession and today's climate it has become an almost losing battle fighting to stay afloat, I have had no regrets in starting my own business as it was a challenge. But as competition and greed starts to get the better of me I wonder how long it will last. Spirit have told me that sooner or later it is inevitable that I will have to take that step into what seems the unknown. Even my so called financial backers in the past have threatened me verbally with taking my house from me to pay back my debts to them, I like many other people have often felt the weight of a cloud over me.

The final decision will not come easy to me, because I always battle through life, striving to reach my goal. If the decision only affected my life it would not be so much of a problem, but it doesn't my wife's failing health and loss of her security is a major worry for me. Where will we live? What will happen to my dogs? Will I be unemployed for the rest of my life? Spirit tell me this, that from the void a new and rewarding life will emerge and I will begin my spiritual working life, free forever of any material worry. A life dedicated to helping others, through their own torment, as a healer, spiritual advisor, philosopher and a speaker. Perhaps access to those people out there who need spirit in their lives. I will be doing this work until I pass into the next and the work will continue forever. Life's eternal flame.

BSE

BSE has been spoken about a lot lately and the media have stirred up a hornets nest. Whether BSE is passed on to humans or not, the most important things are left unsaid, and that is the fundamental rights and welfare or the animals concerned. I'm not sure about the process used in the making of this foodstuff, but I do know this, all ruminants (vegetation eating animals) should never be fed on other animals' parts, this defies nature and BSE is a direct result of this. Pigs eat meat, but if they are fed on the remains of their own species the result could be he same. However with pigs their life span is very short and probably any fault would go undetected. If humans ate one another like the cannibals used to do, the same result would occur. Apart from some farmers no one else seems to care about the actual animals. Cattle have had to pay a very high price for man's stupidity, suffering untold misery and in the end a bullet in the head and burnt in the oven.

These animals are some of God's most beautiful creatures and we must learn from what's happened here. Some people have used what's happened here for political or financial reasons, with a total disregard for life. The killing of cattle over thirty months of age is a total waste of time and life. Efforts should be made into a diagnosis for each animal I'm sure the answer to this is known, each animal found with this disease should be humanely put to sleep and out of the food chain. Spiritual healing for these animals would not work in this instance, because a lesson has had to be learnt by all. The lesson is that man should never under any circumstances interfere with the balance of nature, the consequences of this action always has devastating repercussions. Unfortunately it's always the most vulnerable who get hurt.

Known or Not Known

The answers to all questions are known, but not by us at this moment in time. Phenomenon, paranormal, disease, our future, every single thing that man needs the answers to are known by spirit. It would be too easy for us to have all the answers given to us from spirit now, with no lessons learnt in life. If for example they gave us now the total cure to all cancers what do you think would happen, well I'll tell you, some bright sparks would use the information to their own material advantage and hold the rest of the world to ransom, as would anyone receiving the answers to any other disease, most people always look at what they can make in wealth for themselves. When we can show our true worth with the change in thinking, the answers will be given, Meanwhile the people who can be trusted most are given the opportunity to be the receivers of the healing energies to pass onto others, healing energies that cannot be easily explained by doctors, with a change in thinking you too will be able to heal others including your loved ones, the total change in thinking will come about when all the appropriate lessons have been learnt, now you all know that this is far off in the future.

The answers to anything paranormal or a phenomenon is for all to have now, but only by being spiritual and understanding the spiritual dimension. For myself these two words do not exist, because of the knowledge that I have been given by my spirit guides. If it is your intention to ridicule me, then do so, but I know that sometimes in your spiritual existence you will learn that I'm telling the truth, like spirit I have no reason to lie to you.

Enlightenment

All readers will be touched in some way after reading the contents of this book. If not straight away, then sometime during your life you will be able to reflect back and remember, some will constantly think about the contents and start down their spiritual pathway. Some of you will want to know about spiritual healing, being healed and how to become a healer, if you are one of these people spirit will help you achieve this, whatever happens your life will change for the better from now on. Just by buying this book and reading it this has now put you on hold for further enlightenment. If you want more out of life spiritually speaking then go for it. If you are one of the millions of skeptics, then perhaps this book has touched you in some way, I feel it will be almost impossible for your normal skeptic views to get more hardened after reading this book. Try to understand that spiritual science is only known by the minority at the moment, but sooner than you think by the majority.

Writings

When writing a book on this subject, everything you can think of can be written about. Because spiritual thinking covers all aspects of life. All writings in this book have been chosen by spirit to show the readers the best and the worst of people's thoughts.

Who Cares

These words are often said by people in conversations about one thing or another, with this attitude comes a lowering of your inner self. There have been many tragedies in the world, and some people say 'who cares' if it does not apply to them, well you should care, you should care about all other people in this world. There are religious countries in this world who's soldiers pray as they fire shells from their tanks onto the innocent victims of their intended targets, women and children, the old and infirm, how can people pray to their God and inflict death and terrible injuries on others, something is very wrong here. There are often religious reasons behind wars. If the two sides or more could sit down and say to each other why are we fighting, the real reasons will probably be quite trivial. This non-caring attitude also applies to those of you who hate others because of their colour, what difference does it make the pigment of someone's skin, what difference does it make what religion a person is. What you see and don't like in others is lacking in yourself. You become a mirror image of your own feelings towards others, what you don't like in others is seen by some in you. I can give you an example of this. As I write this chapter I'm sitting in a pub restaurant, waiting for my meal, just before I ordered my meal I canvassed the pub for my business.

While I was eating my meal the telephone rang, the people on the other end were asking the pub to help them in raising funds to give holidays for the handicapped, the owners immediately said no they would not give money to these people, and then on putting the phone down and then in a more raised voice, we do not care we are not carers, on hearing this I said to them well you should care, you should care about these people, nothing was

87

said in reply and you guessed it they did not want me to supply them. The wife of the owner had a problem with her leg and I thought that if they had more of a positive attitude and perhaps had offered a small donation and had asked me to supply them I could have given her direct healing and helped her with her leg. So you can see if you have a more positive attitude how your life could change. Incidentally this pub is one of the wealthiest in the area. I will of course give her absent healing anyway, you see I care.

One Thing Or Another

Truths and untruths were written about earlier, they come however in many disguises. I will mention three examples of this, one Chernobyl, two BSE and three UFO's. The truth of all three is being suppressed. The words first spoken about each subject are normally the honest ones, and then the officials pounce and try their utmost to hide the truth. Chernobyl could not very well be hidden for long, but the truth about the long term outcome is. Many countries in Europe and Scandinavia have been affected by fallout and the ordinary folk have not learnt of the consequences yet. We know about some of what happened in Russia and the rising death rate. Is the food we eat contaminated? If so what will the outcome be. If England is only affected slightly, then what about the European food imports, what will be the worst scenario? All the above as with most things in life are only news for a while, headlines soon revert back to so and so having an affair, if the media looked into more of the untruths, we may start to get some answers.

BSE

An accident waiting to happen, where the greed of man taking short-cuts and endangering a whole animal species in this country, not to mention the possible fatal consequences to man. Animals deserve to be looked after much better than they are. The government says that beef is safe to eat, the government scientists say beef is safe to eat, then if that is the case why is information from two leading men in their own field being suppressed. One man a neurologist and one a doctor. They open their mouths in public and are quickly taken out of the limelight, does the government think that we are all stupid, when there's another fatality some brave soul speaks up again, and again we go around in this endless circle. You so called leaders out there have got to start talking from the heart and reveal all that you are hiding, good or bad. Let us the people decide the consequences of your actions

UFO's

They have been seen in our skies since the time of the caveman, our ancestors only being too aware of flying saucers, as we arrived in them so many years ago. In modern times when most people only dream about them they are still being seen by people from all walks of life every day of the

88

week. They have been landing here since time began and will continue to land here for all time. But this is a subject that is suppressed more than any other, what do they fear perhaps they think that religion will have no more meaning, well they are probably right about that. But it should not bring about a breakdown in our society, but it will start us on that road in a change of thinking and the benefits of us knowing them will be enormous, the technology alone would be worth having. If people from other worlds with their advanced technology beyond our normal thinking have not tried to harm us once, then what's the problem in meeting them. If they come here soon and reveal who they are, they might help us with the repairing of the ozone layer and the rest of this planet, that has been allowed to get into a state of disrepair, to help us get rid of all known pollutants and to show us a form of travel we cannot comprehend. So why have the governments of this world lied to us for so long? Their manifesto's should contain the real truth and why they have kept it from us for so long.

These three subjects are a summary of what is wrong spiritually with this earth, the lies told to us on these subjects and many others. To go forward in life we have to learn to trust one another, and we have got to learn about honesty. Each leader of all the countries of earth no doubt are these kind of people in their own private lives, but they lose their honesty with the affairs of state. Every person on this earth bar none deserve the right to live as free men and women, with dignity honesty and respect for one another, totally free of lies and mistrust. we need people in charge to be honest with us spirit need you to start changing now. Stand out and be leaders of men, lead the country from your heart and not your wallet. You must stop putting a price on everything especially life. If the next spaceship lands near the houses of parliament what are you going to say then, (probably make out it's a television commercial or the filming of E.T. 2).

Part and Parcel

Thought allows us to travel to any distance, we can think of someone, or heal someone who might live on the other side of the world. If we were all telepathic we could all communicate thousands of miles apart. So communication is possible for myself, with like minded people of all planets, thoughts passing through the barriers of time, inter-dimensional thought and inter-dimensional travel. Part and parcel of the same thing.

Does That Make it Right

I'm on holiday again and another year has passed, and yes I'm still writing this book. The day after we arrived at this hotel, we all had that welcome chat and a brief chat about local customs. We were told by our rep that local people had a completely different attitude towards animals than we do, well it's like this the world over. This year I'm in Turkey, and the rep told us

89

that the locals often round up packs of dogs and shoot them. Quite honestly they would be in some cases better off. But I was not to witness any cruelty whatsoever, all the dogs seemed to have been fed with something and there was always some water around, that's not to say that it didn't go on. In my next chapter I'll tell you about something special that took place in Turkey. A lot of the dogs seemed to rely upon the hospitality of the tourists for food titbits, and many Turkish people had their own pet dogs and cats just like us. For the people I did not see being cruel to animals I will say this, that not being cruel shows your true spirituality and for those of you that are cruel to animals it's no good being religious and praying to Allah or your God and then being cruel to your God's creations, it rather makes a mockery of things does it not. Be kind, give food and water to those stray animals even if you can't give them love, these actions alone will earn you great respect from spirit.

Turkish Delight

Today is Wednesday, and I am at the pool side in blistering heat having a cool beer. Suddenly a dog came rushing around the back of the hotel on three legs, the other one hanging limply. Some of the staff were saying that the dog had been hit by a car outside the front of the hotel and that his leg was broken. The hotel chef was in fact the owner of the dog and he was very upset. To my amazement not one person who was sunbathing by the pool got up or inquired about the dog, so much for Turkish customs 'a'. I beckoned the chef to follow me to the side of the hotel and I explained to him that in England I was a healer, and that I wanted to try and heal his dog. After being satisfied that there were no bones broken I gave healing to his leg and the underside of his body, there was a deep gash just below his paw I was concerned that the leaders might have been affected. I told Baram that's the chef that the dog will now sleep for some time and that I expected a recovery. The dog in fact slept for nearly six hours. For the next two days I was not to see Baram or his dog as I was out on trips all day, but on the Saturday morning when I was approaching the pool side bar yet again Baram came running towards me and saying to me the dog, the dog is running again on all four legs, it was wonderful to see him happy it made mine and spirit's day.

Chapter 25: Memories

Who Will Cry For Thomas?

The whole world cries for the children of Dunblane, as we try to reason why this terrible deed should have taken place at all. The children killed, their teacher and their killer, are all together now in spirit. All sharing love and kindness from loved ones who passed over long ago. The love in spirit is equally divided, Thomas Hamilton will be loved none the less. When we search for answers to this terrible tragedy, we must look within ourselves for this is where the answer lies, the warning signs were there for all to see. When Thomas phoned his friend in Kent twice a week and his friend noticed how depressed Thomas was becoming, why did he not offer the hand of friendship? Why did he not invite Thomas over for Christmas so to avoid a lonely Christmas for him? This action alone could have prevented the outcome.

Idle chatter about people you do not know can and does cause tragedies. If a person spends much of his or her life on their own they can have only their selves to talk to, they start to imagine all sorts of things and they in turn get blown out of all proportion. If you live in a community where there are lonely people, and God knows there are millions of them, take the time and trouble to talk to them, even if you have heard something about them that you do not like, on knowing this person better, you will probably find that what was said about them was untrue.

As for Thomas I did not hear anyone at the televised Sunday service say a prayer for him, or give him a mention in a loving Christian way. Thomas being his normal self, would not, in any way have ever contemplated killing children, after all they had played an important part in much of his life. I feel his pain now as he comes to terms with what he has done, he cries out if only somebody loved me. What he is learning now is, that thousands of spirit people love him and always will love him. In his next life when all of this is behind him, he will be given a very loving environment to live in, and he will start on his spiritual pathway in earnest. There is a lesson for every one of us over this tragedy, we must all learn to be compassionate towards our fellow man, and for churches to pray for the victims and assailants and all hope for that better world that is coming.

Chapter 26: Heaven Sent

One - One

There has been many writings, past and present, reflecting feeling of spirituality- Each writer feeling that his or her way is right, and God bless you for this. We are all taught in different ways, some people learn from others, some ancient religions that are in practice today offer help and. guidance to the ill informed. So personal contact with the spiritual dimensions on a one = one basis must be supreme, and we can all have this. First you must look within yourselves. Have you the right make-up to be a writer, and can you understand the power source - for most of the worlds population are in total ignorance of spirituality and what it represents. There need not be any religion of any kind! When spirituality is known by all, it becomes a one - one basis. Why go to church when you could meditate and speak directly with spirit and receive an answer.

I asked and I got

Before I went on holiday I suggested to my guides that if anyone that I met or was near required healing to put them my way. On the aircraft going over to Turkey, a man who was sitting next to me told me that he had a very bad headache, I offered him healing and he accepted and within five minutes all pain had gone. The dog followed the next day and I've already told you about that. The day after that which was Thursday while out on a coach trip, I met a Welsh family. Their daughter was in extreme pain and when the coach made one of its stops I suggested to her mother that I may be able to help her daughter, the daughter was suffering from muscle spasm in her neck, but this offer was flatly refused, they said they did not want to get involved, they were 'chapel you see'.

Nevertheless absent healing was given and a day later I asked the daughter how she was and she said that the pain had improved, that was good enough for me. The same day I met a couple from Dublin and the man was suffering from an injured shoulder and arm, I gave him hands on and absent healing but there was only a slight improvement to come. His wife in a private moment told me that she had been suffering from depression for some time but could not shake it off, and that she wanted a cure without the use of drugs. As it was going to be extremely difficult for me to speak to her at any length I made this suggestion to her. Spirit gave me the words and they told me to tell her this, to offer herself for voluntary work with the old or the handicapped for this is where the answer to her problem lies, on hearing this she said but I will be taking on other people's troubles and that I've got enough of my own. Spirits answer to this was, that other people's problems were no doubt more serious than yours, and a little help and guidance to these people will be an enormous positive step for you and you will find that your life and its purpose will spread out from taking this first step. She told me that she would think about it, at least that's a step in the right direction.

On The Surface

If we could all analyse our thoughts we would find that we think about silly wasteful things during each day. Pettiness towards others, some thoughts quite evil. We need to utilise our thoughts more, to bring about more positive thinking, for example if we corrected our thoughts as we thought of bad things by saying to ourselves no that's not right I should be thinking this, then with plenty of practice we could all start our change in thinking. I have found that by practising what is written here has brought about a dramatic change on my outlook on life. I find that I can forgive others more readily than I could ever have done before. It gradually brings about an inner peace, helping me with my day-to-day worries, you still have them but they are not so important anymore. You tend to smile more often and be generally more happy with yourself. A positive attitude brings many rewards spiritually speaking, it brings you closer to the power source.

Once you can understand your real spiritual self this kind of thinking will come naturally. All living things are spiritual but too many of us love the material and we allow the material to take precedence over life. This change in thought brings about the realisation that everything is just on the surface.

All Good Things Come to an End

You can with the help of spirit write endlessly about life and spiritual matters. But sooner or later we have to come to a conclusion. The conclusion being that I've done my best with the dictation from spirit to inform the readers of a very wide area of knowledge, covering for the first time the very wide areas of spirituality. The writings of other planets is right for this time, and it is time for many myths to be corrected. The whole reality of life is spirituality, we are all spirit in this dimension and all others. We will all have spiritual eternal life, including all living things. As we go forward in time, in say ten years much more knowledge will become available. We will become more aware of spirit and how it affects our lives, so in a few more years people will want to know more, that may be the right time for another book. A book of this sort is rarely written, so we must for now make the most of it.

I will go on learning for the rest of this life, I will learn more about other planets and their people's, I will gradually have a greater understanding of all spirituality. I and spirit have spent more than two and a half years on this book, spirit have been patient and understanding. I would like to thank all my guides and teachers and all my friends from other worlds for helping me. With special thanks to Elijah, Little Bear, Silver Fox, Tei Lei, Tejget, Eeloo, and all the unknown inter-dimensional mediums. Most certainly not the end.

Conclusions

For all the people who may have been mentioned by name, example Robert Maxwell, Lord Longford, William Booth, the members of the royal family any churches or religious groups, spirit and I love you all and we bare no malice towards you. We only point out the good and the bad of any issue, we do not judge you, after all we are all spirits on our spiritual pathways. If a bad point has been made about you or what you represent, then you must look within, the answer is always there, and your spirit guides will be with you all your lives, whether you are bad or good.

I hope that spirit has guided many people into reading this book. I pray that it has enlightened all readers, and that you have received worthwhile knowledge on this subject, it's a subject that you can never tire from talking or reading about. Once read, the contents will never be erased from your minds, it will give you a new goal in life, to work towards. No doubt there will be the skeptics who will think negative thoughts about me and spirit. When I first started writing the book, I felt that some people will ridicule me about the writings. But spirit put my mind at rest by reminding me that these poor souls have got their lessons in life to learn. I will try to answer any questions that are put to me, by any of the readers of this book, and if healing is required I will give it, no matter where you live, by absent healing. All I will require from you is your first name and what is wrong with you. Healing can never be guaranteed, but I will try. If you are taking medicine and seeing a doctor you must continue to do so.

The answer to why animals are spiritually higher than us is this, animals bodily and spiritually live within the balance of nature and we do not. The universe has yet to be discovered. The people that I have had the privilege to talk to, have much knowledge for our world, when the time is right they will impart this knowledge to us.

What's written here is meant as a guide to the perfect spiritual world. This of course will take thousands of earth years, before it becomes fact. In spirit there is no such thing a time, so past, present and future are seen by them.